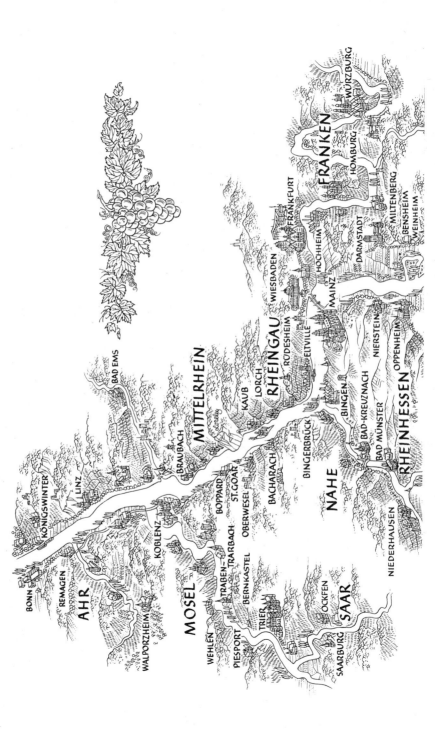

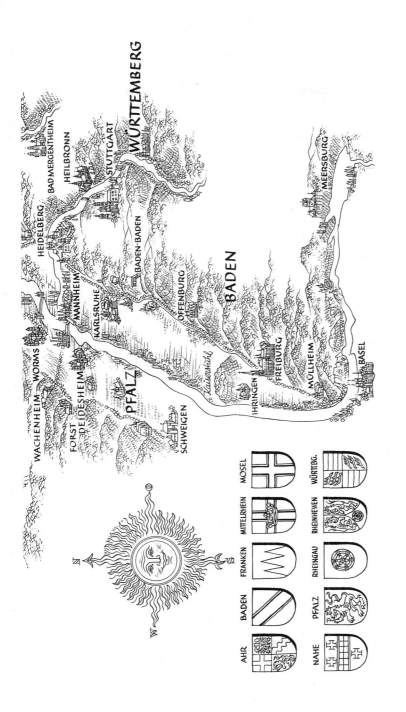

THE WINES OF GERMANY

THE
WINES
OF
GERMANY

BY

FRANK SCHOONMAKER

FRANK SCHOONMAKER'S WINE LIBRARY

HASTINGS HOUSE, PUBLISHERS, NEW YORK

For Cristina

PREFACE TO THE REVISED EDITION

TEN VERY EVENTFUL years have gone by since THE WINES OF GERMANY was first published, and a revised edition would seem, if anything, overdue. Yet as I have gone over its pages, line by line, making such corrections and additions as seemed necessary, I have been surprised, I might almost say comforted, to find how little, rather than how much, the wines themselves and the vineyards that produce them have changed.

Politics and economics, people—and their immense modern appetite for what we call "progress"—have been responsible for all of the major transformations; time, for almost none.

An unhurried traveler on the Moselle, even ten years ago, could almost have taken the famous Latin poem of Ausonius—wine lover, wine grower, and eventually consul—for his guide. The winding, shallow, silvery river, its "vine-clad hills," its fishermen, its barges and sandy beaches and happy villages, which he describes so eloquently, were still there—an odd, timeless fragment of some antique world, although *Mosella* was written in 370 A.D. Today the Moselle is being relentlessly transformed into one of the great commercial waterways of western Europe.

Unfortunately, a whole series of constructive measures, intended to bring the widely varying European wine laws into accord (in the interest of the "Common Market") have for the present been shelved. No doubt they will eventually be adopted and will profoundly alter the whole economy of German wine-growing, and quite possibly some of its nomenclature as well. But this is now for the future.

Meanwhile improved techniques have made possible the earlier bottling and marketing of all German wines, to the great benefit of the less expensive, though perhaps to the detriment of the best. And inevitably, too, there have been changes, in ownership and in comparative class, of some of the great estates.

To bring everything up to date, a certain number of minor corrections have been made in the text of this edition. Matters which required lengthier explanations than space would permit have been covered in a series of *addenda* notes on pages 144-148, and references to these appear in the margin, in each case.

I was, I need hardly say, flattered and gratified to receive, soon after the first publication of THE WINES OF GERMANY, personal letters of praise and encouragement from Chancellor Adenauer and *Reichspräsidenten* Heuss and Lübke, and from Foreign Minister von Brentano. German wines, after two world wars (with Prohibition, in America, almost spanning the gap between the two) had suffered an eclipse: they have at last largely regained the high measure of acceptance which they always deserved among the vintages of the world; this is as it should be.

I have been even more delighted to learn that this small book has turned out to be a sort of minor best seller among Americans stationed in Germany. There is no better bridge between people of good will than good wine, and if THE WINES OF GERMANY has proved in its way an ambassador, it will have accomplished everything I hoped.

—Frank Schoonmaker

New York, January, 1966

ACKNOWLEDGMENT

I SHOULD INDEED COUNT myself ungrateful if I did not say, at the very outset of this little book, that whatever virtues it may possess are in large part due to the counsel and assistance of a number of old friends. When I first began to take something more than a layman's interest in German wines, twenty-odd years ago, I had the great good fortune to fall at once into the hands of the best possible guides, and I am glad to say that when I returned to Germany in 1946, after three years' service in what we used to call the "European Theater of Operations," I found my respect and regard for these particular German friends in no way tarnished or diminished.

Two of the best of them have not lived to see these lines in print, and are citizens today of a country where spring frosts and hailstorms and bad vintages are unknown. In the field of Moselle wines, Otto Dünweg, of Neumagen, was an expert of unique integrity and competence: not reading English with facility, he was kind enough to arrange for two separate translations into German of my chapter on the Moselle, and correct them in his own hand before his death last August. Dr. Wilhelm Bewerunge, of Bonn and Berlin and more recently of Oppenheim, died in November 1954, before I could submit even part of the manuscript for his revisions and suggestions; I am glad to be able to pay him a small tribute by reproducing some of the excellent photographs of vineyards which he himself took with his own camera.

I am also glad to acknowledge a special debt to Josef Becker, of Niederwalluf, unequalled in his knowledge of the Rheingau and a friend of more than twenty years' standing, and to Frau Becker.

However, I should perhaps do an unintended disservice to these friends, as well as to others whom I list below, if I did not say clearly and once for all that the opinions and comparative ratings of districts and towns and vineyards, and vintages, even, were not theirs, but wholly and entirely my own. They are based on twenty-one fairly extended trips through the German wine country in the past twenty-four years in the course of which I tasted (it seems impossible) over seventeen thousand different German wines, of which I have kept a written record of more than half.

This said, I should like to express my gratitude to:

Dr. Albert Bürklin-Wolf, one of the great vineyard owners of the Pfalz and President of the *Verband Deutscher Naturwein-Versteigerer,* the association of German estate-bottlers, who was good enough to read and check my chapter on the Palatinate.

Richard Graf Matuschka-Greiffenklau, owner of Schloss Vollrads and President of the German Wine Producers' Association, who helpfully supplied much important data on the Rheingau.

Herman Franz Schmitt, proprietor of the celebrated Franz Karl Schmitt domain in Nierstein, past President of the Wine Producers' Association of Hessen, whose assistance was particularly valuable in assembling the material for my section on the wines of Hessia.

Dr. Rudolf Gareis, former director of the State Domain in the Rheingau, now retired and living in Eltville, a fountainhead of information and anecdote on the subject of his beloved Rheingau.

Dr. Jost and Dr. Decker, able present directors of the State Domains in the Rheingau and Moselle respectively.

Dr. Krämer and Weinguts-Oberamtmann Karl Nägler of Wurzburg who were both most generous with their help and advice on the subject of Frankenwein, and Steinwein.

Dr. Melsheimer, the leading vineyard owner of Traben-Trarbach on the Moselle.

Dr. von Bassermann-Jordan, dean of German wine-producers, whose books on the history of German viticulture are monuments of thoroughness and scholarship.

Raban Graf Adelmann of Kleinbottwar in Württemberg, and Dr. Villforth of the important State vineyard school at Weinsberg, near Heilbronn, who kindly furnished much information concerning the vineyards of Württemberg, which I knew hardly at all.

Freiherr von Neveu of Durbach, in Baden, who was equally helpful in connection with my all-too-brief study of the vineyards and wines of his native province.

The publisher and the editors of *GOURMET* for permission to reprint certain chapters which appeared, in partial and abbreviated form, in its pages.

Lastly, I should be reluctant to conclude this brief acknowledgment without a word or two of thanks to a great many friends for their hospitality and kindness: Paul and Tatiana Metternich, Herr Labonte, their general manager, and Allinger, who presides over the cellars at Schloss Johannisberg; Jakob Graf Eltz of Eltville, Dr. Weil and Freiherr von Ritter zu Groenesteyn of Kiedrich, the Müller family of the Scharzhof on the Saar and the Rautenstrauch family of Eitelsbach on the Ruwer, the many members of the Prüm clan at Wehlen, young Herr Koch of Wiltingen, Gunther Dünweg of Neumagen, the worthy son of an old friend, and more others than I could possibly here list. They have all helped make the weeks and sometimes months that I have spent in their vineyard country both happy and memorable, which is only fitting, for they all belong to that timeless fraternity of good wine, which has united people of good will in all centuries and in all countries.

—Frank Schoonmaker

Palamós, Spain. April, 1956.

CONTENTS

FOREWORD

THE RHINELANDERS ARE very fond of telling stories about their beloved Chancellor Adenauer. One of the most engaging of these, although possibly aprocraphal, goes like this:

Der Alte (they say) was talking to some friends about the political history of Germany during his lifetime. When he was a young man the management of affairs had been left largely to people from the country of *Schnapps* (spirits)—from Prussia, in other words—with results that were hardly brilliant: the First World War. During his middle years, it had been the turn of people from Bavaria, the land of beer, and the results had been even worse: the Hitler regime, the Second World War, defeat. "Now," he is supposed to have said, "in my old age they call on us—wine drinkers from the Rhine country. Perhaps we shall do better. We could not do worse."

Authentic or not, the story has the ring of truth, and it is certainly a fact that wine drinkers from the German wine country are playing a major role in the Bonn Government. The Chancellor himself is reportedly a discerning judge of wines; the Foreign Minister, von Brentano, comes of a family that has owned vineyards in the Rheingau for generations, and the President of the West German Federal Republic, Dr. Theodor Heuss, although a Württemberger, has an even closer connection with wine-growing and with wine, for he earned his doctorate, some fifty years ago, with a thesis on wine-growing in the Neckar Valley, and now, fifty years later, has written a charming introduction to an excellent new book on German wine.

Keeping pace with Germany's economic recovery as a whole has been the rapid recent growth of an export market for German wines. Precisely as during the years between 1900 and 1914, the United States and Britain have proved by far the most important buyers—Britain for the most part in cask (for tax and customs reasons) and the United States almost entirely in bottle. Actually German wines are now outselling French white wines in the American market, although they bring about as high an average price per case.

Good German wines, such as a large part of those exported, are inimitable and unique. They are the lightest in alcohol of the fine wines of the world and for this reason are never oppressive, never tiring, always refreshing and easy to drink. They go well with food, but on the other hand there is no pleasanter way to enjoy them than outdoors, on a shady terrace, on a warm summer afternoon. The inexpensive ones can be made into all sorts of interesting fruit cups, or *böwle,* or even drunk in the form of a *spritzer,* with soda water, as Lord Byron recommended. The sound, authentic "middle wines," with their bouquet reminiscent of ripe fruit, or wildflowers, their depth of flavor, their cooling freshness on the palate, are a delight, and among the best values in the way of white wines that the world affords. The great wines, the few, true elite, are simply astonishing.

For these, whether they come from Hessia or the Pfalz, from the Moselle or the lordly Rheingau, are, in great years, something almost in the nature of what Robert Louis Stevenson called bottled poetry.

Taste and smell are the beggars among our five senses—they have no true written language and therefore no standards other than wholly personal ones, and no permanent records and no past. They should not necessarily be disprized for that reason: tasting a superlative Moselle can be an aesthetic experience no less genuine than hearing a Mozart concerto well played, or seeing for the first time one of Breughel's paintings. To a person who has no ear for music, a record collector doubtless appears the prince of fools, and there are plenty of people who would gladly pay $10 for a ringside seat at a bull-fight or a prizefight, or three times that for their wife's spring bonnet, who would insist that no bottle of wine ever made was worth one-third as much. Not everyone shares this opinion, fortunately or unfortunately, and the greatest German wines, produced as they are in extremely limited quantities, and only once or twice in a decade, often bring prices that appear fabulous to the uninitiated, who do not realize how much skill and knowledge, yes, and love and care, have gone into their making.

It is a simple fact, and one easy to prove, however, that in the Western World fine wines have been appreciated and prized by the most intelligent and the ablest, the bravest and the most tolerant and the best of every generation for over two thousand years. The wines of Germany's Moselle and Rhine are unsurpassed; they are back on our tables again, and perhaps we can best greet them in the words of Perdita, in *The Winter's Tale* . . .

Reverend sirs, ...
Grace and remembrance be to you both,
And welcome . . . . .

THE WINES OF GERMANY

I

GERMAN WINES

The Land. The Vine. The Vineyards.
The Vintage. The Cellar. The Bottle

A N invisible line, a frontier much more enduring[1] than any national boundary or iron curtain, runs across Western Europe, traced by the sun. It starts north of Nantes on the Atlantic coast of France, parallels the Loire as far as Orléans and continues east to Auxerre, cuts abruptly north to Chateau-Thierry and the Marne hillsides, runs on east to Luxembourg and thence northeast to the Rhine; beyond the Rhine it turns sharply south to Würzburg, Stuttgart and the Black Forest. This line is not, although it sounds like it, a tourist's itinerary —it is the northern limit of the vine.

Beyond this line grapes will not ripen in an average year; along this line, close to it but south of it, are produced the lightest, the most delicate, the most fragrant, the loveliest white wines of the world.

The Moselles and Rhine wines are the undisputed queens among these "border vintages," fine, pale, cold-country wines, so light in

---

[1] This "northern limit of the vine" may be less permanent than it appears. Three hundred years ago the wines of Mantes, northwest of Paris, were among the most famous of France. Wines used to be made in the province of Picardy, due north of Paris, and almost within the memory of man were produced, on a commercial scale, on the slopes of Montmartre, in Paris itself. None of these vineyards exists today although Montmartre has preserved, as a sort of symbol and something of a joke, a tiny plot of Franco-American hybrids. The wine is scarcely one of the principal attractions of Paris.

alcohol that many of them could not legally be classified as wine if they were produced in California. The vineyards from which they come are as far north as northern Newfoundland, almost at the latitude of Winnipeg. There is already snow in the Hunsrück and the Eifel and the Black Forest by the time the grapes are ripe on the lower hillsides in late October; and there is still danger of frost when the first timid leaves appear and the days of the "Ice Saints" come round in early May.

These *Eis-Heiligen,* or Ice Saints, in the German calendar are four: May 12, St. Pancratius; May 13, St. Servatius; May 14, St. Bonifacius; and May 15, *die Kalte Sophie,* or cold St. Sophia. According to tradition, the vines are safe from freezing once these days are past, but a sudden cold snap during the Ice Saints' days has ruined any number of otherwise excellent vintage years. You will see smudge pots out in many German vineyards by May 10, ready to be lighted on short notice if the Ice Saints live up to their reputation, and although they are listed as saints in the calendar, Cold Sophia and her friends are regarded as hardly fit subjects for canonization by the average wine grower.

A hundred days of full sunshine are needed between May and October, the Germans say, to produce good wine, and a hundred and twenty to produce great wine. They get their hundred about every other year, and their hundred and twenty about twice in a decade.

Germany is not, therefore, a wine-producing country in the same sense as Italy and France and Spain. Grapes are grown and wines are made commercially only on a few southern slopes in certain favored valleys. Actually the Bordeaux district of France, with its Graves, Sauternes and Clarets, produces a greater variety of wines than all the vineyards of Germany put together, and the annual production of a single French *département,* the Hérault, is three times that of all Germany. Yet Germany, despite the fact that her wines are limited, in quantity and also in range, ranks, in the special field of fine wines, almost on a par with France.

Leaving out of consideration the German red wines (few of which could be described as fine by the most charitable of judges) it can be said that *all* German wines, from the most inconsequential Gutedels and Kleinbergers of Southern Baden and the Neckar Valley to the noblest and most aristocratic Rieslings of the Rhine, have a decided and unmistakable family resemblance. German vintners, in other words, do only one thing—but they do that one thing supremely well. Germany produces less wine than Chile, but her wines have, beyond any question, a higher average of excellence than the wines of any country in the world.

THE LAND

"Rhineland," says the old German proverb, is "wine-land," and certainly, as far as Germany is concerned, this is gospel. Every German wine of the slightest consequence, from the *Drachenblut,* that rather anemic "Dragon's Blood" which the slopes of *Drachenfels,* near Bonn, yield in the north, to the pleasant little *Seeweine* produced on the shores of Lake Constance on the south, is, in the last analysis, a Rhine wine, or at least a wine produced in the Rhine basin. Not only the Rhine Valley itself, but the valleys of almost all its tributaries, have their wines. Thus the picturesque and charming little valley of the Ahr, which joins the Rhine some twenty miles south of Bonn, has acquired a special and largely local fame for its red wines, which can be most agreeable on a restaurant terrace in summer. The Moselle of course needs no introduction; its waters meet those of the Rhine at Coblenz—the name Coblenz, incidentally, comes directly from the Latin and means confluence. A little farther south, there is the Nahe: along its precipitous and rocky banks are produced a whole collection of wines which are little known outside Germany but which are often admirable. The Main, which gives its name to Mainz (or Mayence) winds down out of the Franconian highlands, by way of Würzburg and Frankfurt; the vineyards of Hochheim, although classified as belonging to the Rheingau, actually overlook the Main, not far from its junction with the Rhine; and along the upper Main are the hills which produce the *Frankenweine* which come to us in the characteristic *Bocksbeutel.* Lastly there is the Neckar, Heidelberg's river, which between Heilbronn and Stuttgart is flanked with vines.

And in addition, of course, in all their unending numbers, there are the wines of the Rhine Valley itself.

Most of this vineyard country, oddly enough, has a trace or a whiff or a what-you-will of Southern Europe in its make-up. The villages are typically and charmingly German, with half-timber houses and high gables, old, painted wrought-iron signs over the tavern doors, ruined castles on a good many of the hills, and window-boxes full of flowers along every main street of every important town. And yet this feeling of the South persists—you will see fig trees and almond trees and apricot trees in the sheltered gardens, and life seems a good deal less rigid and less stern than it is in Prussia. Constantly, and almost everywhere, you will find something reminiscent of Northern Italy or Southern France or Spain, and even now, after eighteen hundred years, something that will make you remember that most of this Rhine country, this vineyard country, was once part of the Roman Empire, influenced by Latin customs and subject to Roman law.

There are the remains of Roman buildings or the relics of Roman life almost everywhere: bronze pruning knives, eighteen centuries old but very like those used today, in a museum; the great dark indestructible mass of the Porta Nigra in Trier; a carved stone signpost across the river from Piesport; a ruined amphitheater; a wine amphora in a private collection; even the Latin names of towns—Cologne, from *Colonia Agrippina,* Mainz, from *Moguntiacum,* Trier, or Trèves, from *Augusta Trevirorum.*

But even more than all these, there is, in the life of this wine country, something ancient and good, a feeling of an old civilization, of well-tilled and well-loved soil.

THE VINE

The Rhine Valley is one of the few, rare districts in Europe where the vine grows wild—as if Nature had set out to prove that the Rhineland had been destined from the beginning to be a "wine-land." This wild vine, however, is of course not the conventional *vitis vinifera,* the "wine-bearer" of almost all European vineyards—it is *vitis silvestris,* much like the familiar *vitis labrusca,* the wild grape of our New England woods. German geologists have even found the clear print of grape leaves in fossils of the tertiary period; these seem to belong to an unknown species which has been christened *vitis teutonica,* and is presumably the earliest German vine. We can safely assume that it was a less good wine grape than the Riesling.

For the *RIESLING,* in Germany, is king. To it, and to it alone, the wines of the Moselle and Saar and Ruwer owe the floweriness of their bouquet and their extraordinary delicacy of flavor. Its tight little bunches of yellow-green grapes, which become deep golden as they ripen, are responsible for practically all the great wines of the Rheingau and the Nahe, and for all the best of those of Hessia and the Pfalz. This may, incidentally, be as good a time as any to point out once more that the name is pronounced *Reece-ling,* not *Rye-sling.*

Even transplanted to other countries, the Riesling preserves a good deal of its astonishing quality and breed. In California it is known as the "white Riesling," or "Johannisberg Riesling," and from it come some of the best wines produced in the country around San Francisco Bay. Its white wine is the finest of Chile, in South America; it is called the "Johannisberg" (presumably after Schloss Johannisberg) in Switzerland, and along the upper reaches of the Rhône Valley, east of Lake Geneva, it yields a few wines not unworthy of the great name they bear. It is grown to a certain extent in the vineyards of Soave, which is perhaps the best of Italian white wines, and in Alsace, of course, overlooking its native Rhine, it is completely at home. There are even unlikely stories to the effect that one or two of the better Graves, in the Bordeaux Country, owe their finesse to a proportion of Rieslings planted among the Semillons and Sauvignons which predominate in their vineyards.

Despite this ability to survive and prosper in other countries, the Riesling is at its best in Germany, as no one who has ever tasted a great Scharzhofberger, or a great Marcobrunner, or a Forster Kirchenstück, can for a moment doubt. This, of course, is partly a matter of climate (the Riesling does not like weather overly hot or extremely dry), partly a matter of soil (the Riesling shows a marked preference for steep, unfertile hillsides and for stony ground), and partly a matter of the loving care with which the vine is cultivated and with which the grapes are picked and sorted and pressed. Such loving care the Germans give to the Riesling, full measure and running over. And what the Riesling gives in return is beyond praise.

Surprisingly enough, vastly more German wine is made from other, more productive, less distinguished grapes than from the Riesling itself. Most of these have the virtue of a higher yield per acre, plus an ability to do well on heavier or partially alluvial soil. The most popular and one of the best of them (and a very good grape too) is the *SYLVANER*. This, like the Riesling which it in no way resembles, has a confusing multiplicity of names. In the Rheingau, where it is little grown, it is called the *Oesterreicher*, which would seem to indicate that it originated in Austria. In the Pfalz it goes by the name of the *Franken Traube,* or "Franconian Grape," and predominates in all of the secondary vineyards, as indeed, under its proper name, Sylvaner, it does in Hessia. Around Würzburg, in Franconia, the Steinwein country, it is sometimes even called the "Franken Riesling"—but this name is almost in the nature of a joke, like Welsh Rabbit or Scotch Woodcock. However, in the United States, the Sylvaner has had the effrontery to call itself simply

"Riesling," instead of "Franken Riesling," and this absurd misnomer has received, alas! official sanction, so that in order to get a true Riesling wine from California, the consumer now has to ask for "Johannisberg Riesling." It would be hard to find a more illegitimate appropriation of a great name. It is also rather amusing to note that Swiss usage is the exact opposite of American in this connection: a Swiss wine labeled "Johannisberg" may be made from either Sylvaner or Riesling; one labeled "Riesling" may be made only from the true Riesling grape.

Sylvaner wines on the whole mature more quickly, have less substance and body, and infinitely less class than Rieslings. If they are proportionately less expensive, as they should be, they can be recommended, for they are admirable everyday wines, quite drinkable when only a few months old.

Some twenty or thirty other varieties appear on the official roster of German wine grapes, but most of these are of more interest to the botanist than to anyone else. Here are a few exceptions:

Klevner (Pinot Blanc). Good, but not widely cultivated.

Ruländer (Pinot Gris). Excellent. Yields some good wines in Baden and Württemberg, as indeed it does in Alsace.

Traminer, or *Gewürztraminer.* Excellent. Celebrated in Alsace, produces a few unusual and highly aromatic wines in the Pfalz. Incidentally, Gewürztraminer means "spicy" Traminer.

Müller-Thurgau. This is a fairly recent cross of the Riesling and Sylvaner, and takes its name from its originator. It is extremely productive, does well on heavy soil, and yields a pleasant, mild, short-lived wine of good bouquet and rather low acidity.

Gutedel. Called the Fendant in Switzerland and the Chasselas in France. Productive. In Germany, yields wines of secondary quality and not much flavor.

Elbling, or *Kleinberger,* or *Rauschling.* Grown in mediocre vineyards at the upper and the lower end of the Moselle. Also in Württemberg and Baden. Poor.

Spätburgunder (Pinot Noir). One of the very greatest of all red-wine grapes. For additional information, see the section on German Red Wines.

THE VINEYARDS

The vineyards of Germany are very ancient. Many of them, certainly those of the Moselle and of Hessia and the Pfalz, date back to the dawn of the Christian era, a century or so after Caesar's conquest of Gaul. At the beginning, their expansion was limited by very severe laws forbidding the planting of the vine in Roman colonies—perhaps the first but certainly far from the last protectionist legislation in the field of wine. These laws were finally abrogated in the third century A.D. by the Emperor Probus, who is today regarded as the father of German viticulture, although whether he ever tasted a glass of German wine is at least doubtful.

In any case, a hundred years later, the Latin writer Ausonius, who gave his name to Chateau Ausone, in France, published a famous descriptive poem about the *Mosella* and its wines, and many of the Roman relics that have been unearthed date from approximately the same period.

There exist dozens of stories and legends about these historic vineyards, but it is a little difficult to say how many of them are worthy of credence. Thus it is told that Charlemagne, from the great palace which he built at Ingelheim on the Rhine near Mainz, perceived that there was one slope across the river, in what is now called the Rheingau, on which the snow melted earlier than elsewhere; he ordered that it be planted with vines, and this is now the steep vineyard of Schloss Johannisberg.

As everywhere in Europe, the early history of the vineyards is closely bound up with the history of the Church and of the monastic orders, particularly the Cistercians and the Benedictines. A surprisingly high proportion of the great German vineyards were created by monks and were at one time ecclesiastical property; despite the fact that most of these holdings have long since been secularized, it is still possible to buy a wine (and a very good wine, too) produced and bottled by the Cathedral of Trier.

An outline map of Western Germany, showing only the rivers, is surprisingly like a wine map of the same country. There are differences, of course. The Rhine, north of Bonn and south of Worms, runs in general through flat land unsuited to vines. But German vineyards, as a whole, are river vineyards and hillside vineyards; in this northern latitude the grape requires a maximum of sun, which only a hillside vineyard, facing south, can provide, and most such

slopes are along river valleys. The majority of German vineyards, for
the same reason, are steep, and have to be created, cultivated and
maintained by hand labor.[2] Each individual vine, on the Moselle, has
its stake, taller than a man; along the Rheingau and in Hessia and
the Pfalz, the vines are strung on wires and tailored until they look
like hedges in a formal garden.

An inconceivable amount of care goes into the selection of the
vines themselves. Along the Moselle you will see colored rings, quite
often, painted on the vine stakes; these, like ribbons at a dog show,
are the marks of a champion, a particularly sturdy or particularly
productive vine, and it is from these that cuttings are taken for
propagation.

Like practically all the wine-producing vines of France, those of
Germany are for the most part grafted, and on "American" roots.
In the latter half of the last century, an insect pest invaded Europe
from the United States, probably carried on some native American
grape cuttings brought over for experimental purposes. The name of
the pest is *phylloxera vastatrix*; it is a tiny louse which lives on the
roots of vines; in the Eastern United States, where the roots of the
hardy native vine are tough, it survives without destroying. In Europe
(as in California where the vineyards are planted with European
varieties) its arrival was a major catastrophe; it devastated and destroyed three-quarters of the famous vineyards of the world in the
space of less than fifty years. The remedy was found at last—to bring
over to Europe, and from the Eastern States into California, the wild,
native American vine, or some hybrid descended from it, and to graft
on this resistant stock the Rieslings, the Sylvaners, etc., which, *unlike
the wild American vine*, produce grapes for fine wine.

Although Germany produces a far higher proportion of fine
wine, as compared with cheap and ordinary wine, than any other
major country, there is plenty of the latter. Certainly not over a fifth
of Germany's wine could be considered fit for export, even if a foreign
market existed for it, and even if the thirsty Rhinelanders did not
drink it up themselves. The superior vineyards, with which this book
is principally concerned, are surprisingly limited in extent; the biggest
of them is tiny in terms of an American farm: including the best as
well as the worst, there are less than 5600 acres under vines in the

---

[2] There is an old wine-growers' proverb that tells us, *"Wo ein Pflug kann
gahn, soll kein Rebstock stahn!"*, or "Where a plow can go, there no vine should
grow."

whole Rheingau, and the internationally famous Steinberg, for example, consists of under 65 acres of sloping and priceless ground.

Here are a few statistics which will perhaps make the picture even clearer.

As of a year ago there existed in all of Western Germany approximately 135,000 acres of producing vineyard; at the same time there were more than 150,000 vineyard owners; the average holding, therefore, consisted of less than a single acre of vines, and an acre, in an average year, yields in the neighborhood of 500 gallons, or roughly 2500 bottles of wine.

The Pfalz, or Palatinate, is the largest wine-growing district of Germany, with some 35,000 acres under vines, and an average annual production of nearly 15,000,000 gallons. Apart from growers' co-operatives, there are 42 vineyard-owners grouped in an association of quality wine producers, and these 42 produce half or more than half of all the fine wines of the Pfalz. *And yet the total holdings of these 42 "great" growers amount to only 1054 acres in all.* Perhaps the most famous of these estates is that of Dr. Bassermann-Jordan, whose name, like his charming, old-fashioned label, is known to wine lovers in every country on earth. This estate consists of 90 acres of vines— divided into more than fifty separate holdings in as many different vineyard plots, each one legally delimited, and having its own traditional and well-established name.

Similarly, one of the greatest vineyard properties of the Moselle is that of the Catholic Seminary, the Bischöfliches Priesterseminar, of Trier. This consists of roughly 70 acres of vines, divided into over twenty different holdings in eight different parishes or townships, and the total production amounts to some 200 casks, or Fuders, of wine a year. When it is kept in mind that each one of these casks will be marketed under the precise name of the township *and* the vineyard plot from which it comes, it is obvious that we are not dealing with something produced in industrial quantities.

The major vineyard districts of Germany, their acreage under vines and their approximate average production are as follows:

Moselle-Saar-Ruwer. Some 20,000 acres, of which less than one-third produce wines of superior quality. Total yield about 10,-000,000 gallons.

Rheingau. Some 5500 acres (although only 4200 in full production) perhaps two-thirds of which could be called good. Average yield about 2,250,000 gallons.

Hessia. Some 31,000 acres, of which only about 4000 are in the eight townships which produce wines of top quality. Total yield about 13,000,000 gallons.

Nahe. Some 4500 acres, perhaps a quarter of them above average. Yield about 2,000,000 gallons.

Pfalz. Some 35,000 acres, not over one-tenth of which produce superior wine. Average yield about 15,000,000 gallons.

Franconia. Some 7000 acres, less than 10% superior. Average yield about 2,000,000 gallons.

Baden and Württemberg. Some 33,000 acres, less than 2% producing superior wine. Total yield about 14,000,000 gallons.

THE VINTAGE

The Riesling and Sylvaner are both grapes which the professional likes to describe as "precocious"—they mature early, and in California, for example, they are generally the first to be picked. But in Germany, the vintage, or harvest, rarely begins before mid-October, and in certain extraordinary years it continues through November, long after the wine has been pressed out and fermented and safely stored away in its cellar in other countries. The truth is, of course, that most grapes other than the Riesling and the Sylvaner would simply not ripen at all in the pale, cool autumn sunshine of the Moselle and Rhine.

This question of ripeness is an exceedingly important one: in the field of German wine, it is the key to everything—to vintage charts and vineyard ratings, to nomenclature, and even price. The most expensive wines are those made from grapes that are not only ripe, but over-ripe; the cheapest from grapes so green and sour that sugar has to be added to their juice in order to produce something that can pass for wine. The "great" vintage years are those in which a high proportion of grapes achieve full maturity, just as the "great" vineyards are those favored slopes on which the grapes ripen more often and more completely than on neighboring hillsides.

The gradations of ripeness are many, but they are on the whole pretty clearly defined. Lowest in the scale are the grapes (and the

wines they yield) to which sugar has to be added. In a disappointing
year such as 1960, nine-tenths of all the wine that Germany produces
may fall into this category. At the same time, there are vineyards,
many of them, so ill-favored and poor that they are incapable of
producing good *natural* (in other words, unsugared) wine, even in the
greatest years. And finally, there may be, for example, two growers
with holdings side by side: one of them, fearing a break in the
weather, and rain, will decide to pick early—his grapes will not be
altogether ripe and his wine will have to be sugared. Meanwhile his
more adventurous neighbor may have decided to gamble, to leave his
grapes on the vine—if he is lucky he will need no beet sugar or cane
sugar, for he will have in its place the natural and far superior sweetness of the grape itself. Thus of two Niersteiners of the same year,
grown within fifty feet of one another, one may be sugared and the
other a *Naturwein* or "natural" wine.

It should be pointed out that there is nothing wrong or repre-
hensible or illegal about this "sugaring" process; the practice is an
accepted and a common one, not only in Germany but in France
(where it is called *chaptalization,* after Chaptal, Napoleon's Minister
of Agriculture), and in the Finger Lakes district of New York State.
In the majority of cases, the sugar (its amount limited by law) is
added, not to wine, but to the grape juice before fermentation, and its
purpose is not to make the wine sweet but to give it the necessary
minimum of alcohol. Were it not for sugaring, thousands of tons of
grapes would be wasted in poor years, instead of being made to yield
something which is wholly potable, generally inexpensive, and in many
instances far from bad.

See
note
1-1

It goes without saying that to sell sugared wine as natural wine
is flagrant dishonesty and is considered fraud in most wine-producing
countries. *Providing he knows what to look for on a German wine
label* (and few people do), a consumer can distinguish between the
two almost infallibly. This rather thorny question will be discussed
fully, as it deserves to be, in the next chapter.

The next step up in the scale of ripeness, and a long step it is
too, is the normally ripe grape which gives a sound and good wine
without anything in the way of an assist from a sugar refinery. Such
grapes make up the bulk of the crop from better-than-average vineyards in better-than-average years. But there are other and higher
rungs on the ladder.

For at this point, beyond what might be called the normal ripening brought about by sunshine and warmth, there is another factor

that enters the equation. This is the so-called "Noble Mold" (technically *botrytis cinerea*) which the Germans call *Edelfäule* and the French *la pourriture noble*. Long before the discovery of penicillin, German and French vintners, like the makers of Roquefort and Camembert cheese, had learned that some molds are not only harmless but extraordinarily beneficent and useful—without *botrytis,* neither the great Sauternes of France nor the great Moselles and Rhines of Germany would be what they are.

The Noble Mold comes late in the season, and it exists only in a few vineyard districts, generally in those where September and October are months of warm days and cool nights with heavy dew and a good deal of fog.[3] It appears first as a gray down, hardly more than a shadow, on the ripening grapes; gradually, through its action, the grapes tend to become shrunken and their skins almost transparent—the water in their juice evaporates while their sweetness and flavor become more and more concentrated. At the end, even whole bunches are covered with the gossamer of the mold: shriveled, discolored, to the unpracticed eye they look anything but appetizing or attractive, but from such grapes are made the rarest and the most expensive of all white wines.

All sorts of stories are told, both in Germany and in France, about the discovery of the effects of *botrytis,* for this was almost certainly accidental.

Many years ago, they say, when most of the great Rheingau vineyards were still Church property and their cultivation carried on by monks, the Bishop of the nearby town of Fulda was required, every year, to give his official consent before the grape harvest could begin. One particular fall (and as to the year the chroniclers are a little vague)[4] a messenger was dispatched as usual to Fulda when the grapes were ripe. On his way he was set upon by robbers and failed to return. After an anxious fortnight had gone by, and the grapes were becoming over-ripe, a second messenger set out for Fulda. He too disappeared. Finally, as his beloved grapes became more and more gray and apparently withered, the despairing Abbot sent a third courier, who at last brought the Bishop's authorization. Although convinced that his crop was a total failure, the Abbot decided to

---

[3] 1947 was one of the driest years of the last half century in Germany and in general the Noble Mold never appeared at all. The wines had plenty of alcohol and body, but they were a great deal less fine than they would have been if the *Edelfäule* had been there to do its work.

[4] There is some evidence that would lead us to believe that this happened in 1783. It was certainly in the latter half of the 18th century.

salvage what he could, and sent his pickers into the vines. To his astonishment, and that of everyone in the Rheingau, the wine was the best that had ever been made.

We know a great deal more about the Noble Mold[5] today than the Bishop of Fulda and his Abbot, but we are a long way from knowing everything about it. We have learned what conditions are favorable to its appearance and its development, and something of how it works its miracles on the ripening grapes, but of where it comes from and why, we are as ignorant as ever.

In good years, grapes that are harvested late have of course a higher proportion of bunches that have been touched by the Noble Mold than grapes harvested early, and of course, quite apart from the Mold, they are sweeter and riper. Vineyard owners who are willing and able to afford the risk will therefore often delay picking for a period of days and even weeks after the vintage has officially begun— a date which varies from year to year and is set by a local committee of producers and experts. Again they may harvest part of the crop at the normal time, and send their pickers through the vines not once but even three or four or five times. Granted good weather, wines from the later picking (*Spätlese*) are of markedly superior quality, softer, finer and a little less dry, and they command, as indeed they should, a higher price.

In an effort to achieve something even better, the German vintners have devised a whole series of special techniques and stratagems which they employ at vintage time. Almost every one of these involves a vast amount of additional and highly specialized work, and most of them entail as well a considerable sacrifice in the total quantity of wine produced.

Practically all of the better growers, for example, *deliberately* produce, in a given vineyard and a given year, three or four or even more quite different and wholly dissimilar wines. One (or in some instances several) of these will be a wine or wines made quite simply from grapes that are normally ripe; one or more will be a *Spätlese,* from grapes that have been allowed to hang on the vines to get the benefit of an additional fortnight or month of autumn sunshine, and one, at least, will be an *Auslese,* literally a "selection."

[5] The Noble Mold almost certainly exists in the United States: its presence has been reported and I think confirmed in the Finger Lakes District, and I myself have seen what I believe to be *botrytis* in the Santa Cruz Mountains of California. It is extremely doubtful, however, that wines made from grapes with the Noble Mold will be produced in America in the foreseeable future— far too much hand labor is involved to render them commercially possible.

This *Auslese*, which is a wine a good deal sweeter and a great deal more expensive than what might be called the run of the mine, is made entirely from bunches that have been selected as they were picked as being either especially ripe or touched more than the average by the Noble Mold. Obviously, a grower who uses all such grapes in the making of *Auslese* wines sacrifices thereby the general quality of his crop; the ideal is to strike a fair and good balance, a few casks of *Auslese* for the connoisseurs' great occasions, and perhaps ten times as many casks of good and sound wine for general sale.

See note 1-2

But there are even further refinements. The greatest and most expensive German wines of all, and they are both astonishingly great and fabulously expensive, are almost in the nature of dessert wines. Like the famous Sauternes, like Château d'Yquem, for example, they are far too sweet to be drunk straight through a meal; one glass of them, in general, is enough, but even one glass is an experience.

These are the *Beerenauslesen* and *Trockenbeerenauslesen*— *Auslese*, as before, meaning a selection, and *Beeren* meaning berries or individual grapes, and *trocken*, of course, meaning dry or dried. These quite incredible names are wholly descriptive and wholly accurate, for such wines are indeed made out of grapes that have been picked one by one, with the aid of a tiny scissors or a needle, grapes completely covered with the Noble Mold or grapes that have almost turned to raisins on the vine. During the *Lese*, or grape harvest, these are carefully placed in special little pannikins, clipped to the shallow wooden buckets into which the pickers put their grapes. They are pressed separately and fermented separately, and although the best wines so made sometimes bring prices of $20 or even $40 or more per bottle, their production is not infrequently quite as much a matter of pride as it is of profit. These extraordinary golden nectars are made, quite literally, drop by drop.

As in all wine-producing countries, the vintage season in Germany, particularly if the quality is good, is a time of general gaiety and rejoicing. There are festivals in the vineyard towns, and more than once in the soft October dusk, I have seen loaded ox-carts coming back from the vines, the pickers singing as they followed, and the oxen themselves garlanded with grape leaves. In this atmosphere of bounty and gratitude and good cheer it is all too easy to forget the devotion and skill and endless labor which have made the harvest possible, and the risks and complexities of the harvest itself. Every cart that rolls so happily and so easily toward press and cellar is really in the nature of a little victory, won against heavy odds in a long battle in the most difficult wine-producing country in the world.

THE CELLAR

From a purely technical point of view, German cellars on the whole are better equipped than those of any other wine-producing country. There are a great many large producers, and most of the small ones (generally referred to as *Winzer,* or wine-growers, as distinguished from *Weinbaubesitzer,* or vineyard-proprietors) have banded themselves together into co-operatives. The State has done its part through the creation of viticultural stations and excellent technical schools, and German industry has contributed all sorts of remarkable inventions in the way of presses, filters and special fermenting tanks, insecticides for the vines and methods of clarification, which even France would do well to copy.

Even since the last War, great changes have taken place in German wine-making methods. Some of these have surprised and perhaps shocked the old-fashioned, but certainly their general effect is all to the good (the consumer's good). The principal trend, like that in France and in America, is all in the direction of younger wines, wines that can be consumed in all the fruit and freshness of their youth, after eighteen months or two years rather than after five or ten. Naturally such wines are on the whole less expensive; it is possible that they will never achieve quite those extraordinary peaks of excellence which made the fame of the 1893's, the 1911's, the 1920's and the 1921's (although having tasted all of these, and more recently the 1949's and 1959's, I am inclined to doubt it). Almost certainly they will be shorted lived. But the difference, I am convinced, is a net gain.

Cellar methods differ to a certain minor degree from one German district to another, but much less than they did fifty years ago. In general the grapes come direct from the vineyard to the press-house, although sometimes, if the distance is too great, they are stemmed and crushed into a cask on an ox-cart along the roadside. When they reach the *Kelterhaus,* they are pressed as soon as possible in hydraulic presses[6] (the juice from the last pressings being

---

[6] A sensational new press, the *Willmes Presser,* developed since the War, is rapidly replacing the standard hydraulic press in most of the better German cellars. It consists of an elastic, plastic sleeve, inside a stainless steel cylinder,

of course kept separate) and the resulting *Most,* or must, is set to ferment.

The barrels, or casks, in which this fermentation takes place, and in which the wine is stored for aging after fermentation, vary quite surprisingly from one district to another in Germany. On the Moselle, the traditional and universal cask is the *Fuder,* of somewhere between 960 and 1000 liters capacity; in terms of bottles, it is generally estimated at 1300, or 108 cases, give or take a few bottles, and it is in terms of *Fuders* that almost all Moselle wines are sold by the producers.

In the Rheingau, and in Hessia, the unit is the *Halbstück* (literally the half-piece—although in France a *pièce* is a barrel, generally one of just over 50 gallons). A *Halbstück* is a cask of 600 liters—it gives approximately 800 bottles or about 68 cases.

Still another standard of measurement is used in the Palatinate, or Rheinpfalz. Here, just as in Alsace to the south, the casks are usually considerably larger, often oval rather than round, and in size they range anywhere from about 600 liters (roughly 160 gallons) to six or seven times that size. The wines are sold, before bottling, in units of 1000 liters, a rather arbitrary standardization made necessary by the widely varying size of the barrels. These 1000-liter lots are often referred to as *Fuders* even when the wines in question are stored in much larger or much smaller casks.[7]

Needless to say, good German cellars are cool—I have seen the thermometer reading 54° in a cellar in Bernkastel in mid-August when it was well over 90° in the vines, fifty feet from the cellar door. In cellars less cool, German wines could not conceivably preserve the freshness, the pale green-gold color, the lightness and fruitiness which make their charm. Nor would they preserve these qualities if they were not scrupulously cared for. In a cellar used

---

mounted horizontally on a metal frame which, in turn, is on rollers. When the sleeve is inflated (just as the inner tube of a tire is inflated) and the cylinder slowly revolved, outward pressure is exerted on the grapes, and the juice passes through hundreds of narrow slits in the cylinder's surface, into a stainless steel trough mounted directly below it. Being on rollers, the press can be moved around the press-house as easily as a piece of furniture.

[7] In the past four or five years some exceedingly interesting experiments have been carried on involving the use of glass-lined steel tanks rather than wooden casks. The results have been so encouraging that such tanks have actually been installed at Schloss Johannisberg and in the great State-owned establishment where Steinberger is produced. It seems at least possible that within a decade or two, all of those picturesque and shining casks, which have been the glory of German cellars until now, will have disappeared.

for the maturing of fine wine, perfect cleanliness is as necessary as in a hospital. The casks have to be kept brim full, and are checked at least once a week. The wine, at certain stages in its development, has to be "racked"—siphoned off from one cask to another, leaving the sediment or "lees" behind. Then at the proper time it has to be clarified, or "fined."

This is a process almost as old as wine-making itself. Just as farmers used to drop eggshells into the coffeepot "to make the grounds settle," so there are certain products which, stirred into a cask of wine, will form an invisible, tenuous network in the wine, and settle, carrying the sediment to the bottom and leaving the wine brilliant and clear. Whites of eggs, for example, have been used for this purpose for centuries, especially for red wines, and the Germans have developed other very special clarifying agents which are of more interest to the wine chemist than to the consumer. These do their work extremely well, for sediment, in a German wine, is almost unknown, and a bottle with even a trace of cloudiness ranks as an extraordinary exception.

During the months following fermentation, particularly once they have "fallen bright" and been racked for the first time, light white wines like those of the Moselle and Rhine change and develop quickly: they lose the characteristic yeastiness of unfinished wine, they begin to acquire bouquet, their initial "greenness" disappears. Naturally the "little" wines that are destined to be short-lived pass through the diverse stages of their evolution more rapidly than their fuller-bodied and finer contemporaries. But for one and all there comes a day, perhaps after only seven or eight months, perhaps after eighteen, when the cellar-master tastes them again and pronounces them *abfüllfertig*—ready for the bottle. Long before this graduation day, the unworthy will have been eliminated: the poorly balanced will have been shipped away to some blending cellar, the small and unpromising to be served by the carafe or glass in the local *Weinstuben;* only those considered fit to receive the diploma, in the form of a branded cork, an estate label and an honored name, are still in the cellar on their bottling day.

THE BOTTLE

Germany has given us two basic patterns in the way of wine bottles— one, of course, is the familiar, slender, long-necked *Flasche,* the traditional bottle of the Moselle and Rhine; the other is the amusing

Bocksbeutel, the round-bellied flagon used for the *Steinweine,* the wines of Franconia, and occasionally for certain of those of Baden. Both are attractive, and both have been used for supposedly similar but often quite dissimilar wines, in countries all the way from Italy and Spain to Chile and California.

Let us confine ourselves, for the moment, to the standard bottle; it contains about three-quarters of a quart (roughly .72 liters); it is green on the Moselle, brown in the Rheingau, Hessia and the Pfalz (though, oddly enough, green in Alsace). A few very cheap wines are shipped in liter-bottles (just over a quart) of the same form, but I do not recall having seen these outside of Germany. German bottles are filled very full, sometimes so that there is hardly a perceptible bubble of air next to the cork, and it is decidedly risky to store them in a warm place, since the natural expansion of the wine will, under such conditions, sometimes push up the cork.

The corks come mostly from Spain and Portugal. They are generally shorter than those used in France (the wines being sooner ready and on the whole shorter-lived), and most of them are branded with the name and sometimes with the coat-of-arms of the producer. As a matter of fact, you will rarely see an unbranded cork in a superior bottle of German wine.

Even when the wine is *abfüllfertig,* or ready for bottle, it invariably requires a little final processing, usually in the form of filtration. The Germans are past masters in the field, and the great Seitz factory in Bad Kreuznach on the Nahe, completely rebuilt since the War, has made some astonishing contributions to this rather exact science. In the last four or five years, progress has been particularly rapid, and a method known as "sterile-bottling" has not only been introduced, but actually adopted by a majority of progressive vineyard owners. Considering how reluctant wine-makers generally are to abandon the traditional ways of their fathers, this amounts almost to a revolution. More than any other thing, it has made possible the early bottling and early marketing of white wines, with no loss and in some cases an actual gain in quality.

The wine, when "sterile-bottled," is run through an exceedingly fine filter, which not only removes all traces of sediment, but actually all yeast cells which might conceivably produce a later, secondary fermentation and clouding. The bottles are sterilized, and the corks. All this is done without Pasteurization (which of course involves heating the wine and is highly detrimental to its quality).

It is such wines that Germany is able to send us today, and they are in every sense the result of the best possible combination of a respect for tradition and a willingness to accept all that modern science has achieved in the past fifty years. They are not the product of primitive farms and they are not the product of factories—they are wines made with care, with intelligence and with love.

II

NOMENCLATURE

German Wine Labels and What They Mean

TO the uninitiated layman, the label on a really distinguished bottle of German wine (or on one that pretends to be) appears at first sight about as intelligible as so much Sanskrit. In most cases, it is quite attractive, with a landscape or an old coat-of-arms in color (which may be the coat-of-arms of the producer and may not); next comes a vintage year (probably a good one, possibly a poor one) followed by a series of three or four fairly long German words, all of them unfamiliar, and finally the name of some institution or individual or corporation which may be anything from a count to a cathedral, from a peasant wine-producer to a large commercial wholesaler of wines and spirits. After one or two encounters with this sort of problem, most people fall back on something called Liebfraumilch or Moselblümchen, and no wonder.

To do so, however, is to miss entirely the wines that have made the international fame and glory of German vineyards, and these are certainly among the greatest white wines in the world. As a matter of fact, German wine labels are not as complicated as they look—they are very like what youngsters used to call "pig Latin" . . . you have to learn a trick or two, and the rest is easy. Once you can read them, they turn out to be the most accurate and informative wine labels that exist, for they give you the background and tell you the life story of what you are about to drink in terms which are a model of directness and precision.

Almost all of the fine wines of Germany (like almost all of the fine wines of France) bear names that are geographical in origin— the name of the village from which they come, or that of a particularly famous vine-covered hillside, or that of a castle which overlooks the vineyard. There are a few extremely important exceptions, and since such exceptions unfortunately make up a very large part of the wines that Germany exports today, we may perhaps best deal with these, before returning to the more specific and accurate labels which all those who know and who love German wines vastly prefer, for the best of reasons.

These non-geographical appellations, which the Germans call *Fantasie-Namen,* or "invented names," include such old favorites as Liebfraumilch, Moselblümchen, and the like, as well as others which are proprietary—in other words, brand names which are the legal property of some bottler or exporter. There is nothing in the slightest wrong or improper about such names, except the fact that they are meaningless, or almost so. Some of the best Rhine wines of Germany can legally be shipped as Liebfraumilch . . . but so can the worst. A bottle marked Moselblümchen *may* contain pure, unblended Wehlener Sonnenuhr Auslese, but the chances are at least 50,000 to 1 against, and the probability is that it will be some blend of artificially sweetened wines from third class vineyards. In any case, the consumer cannot tell, and the label does not give him the information to which he is properly entitled. Some very fine wines are unquestionably shipped as Liebfraumilch, but all of us would be happier if they were labeled Niersteiner, or Oppenheimer, or Nackenheimer, after the town they come from. At least we could thus tell them apart from the myriad Liebfraumilchs which come from the secondary wine-producing townships where no one has ever made a fine wine and no one ever will.

Let us come back, after this minor detour, to the authentic and legitimate German wine labels which tell a complete and an honest story—they may be attractive or may not, but they are at least unfailingly informative. This is what they tell you, or are supposed to tell you:

1. To begin with, they tell you where the wine comes from. Generally speaking, this is a village, and the name of the village is the name of the wine. Just as a man from New York or London is a

New Yorker or a Londoner, so a wine from Rüdesheim is a Rüdesheimer, a wine from Nierstein is a Niersteiner and a wine from
Piesport is a Piesporter. A few great castles and a few extraordinary
vineyards are more famous and more important than the townships
in which they lie, and these give the vineyard name, *rather than the
township name,* to the wines which they produce. Thus we have
Schloss Johannisberger (from Schloss Johannisberg), Steinberger
(from the Steinberg vineyard, near Hattenheim), Scharzhofberger
(from the Scharzhofberg, near Wiltingen, on the Saar), and so on.
But these are exceptions, and the basic rule holds true.

In every important wine-producing township there are a number
of vineyards which have acquired, over a period of centuries, or at
least decades, a special reputation for quality. Wines from such
superior vineyards are invariably sold under *the vineyard name in
addition to the town name,* as Rüdesheimer Schlossberg, Niersteiner
Auflangen or Piesporter Goldtröpfchen. It is safe to assume that any
German wine which does *not* carry a specific vineyard name is an
inferior wine; it is probably a blend; it certainly does *not* come from
a top vineyard. In certain instances, it should be noted, what appear
to be vineyard names are actually nothing of the sort, but brand or
generic designation; these will be discussed in detail further on.

See
note
2-1

The names of the genuine little vineyard plots, or *Lagen,* are
usually very old, and sometimes both picturesque and descriptive.
There are literally hundreds if not thousands of them, and in many
of them are combined some fairly common word, and some purely
local designation. Thus one runs across, over and over again, vineyard names that end or start with *Berg* (hill), *Baum* (tree), *Burg* or
Schloss (castle), *Bach* (stream), *Brunnen* (fountain or spring), *Dom*
(cathedral), *Kirche* (church), *Kloster* (monastery or convent), *Hof*
(court or manor-house), *Garten* or *Gärtchen* (garden, or little garden), *Kreuz* (crucifix), *Mauer* (wall), *Pfad* or *Weg* (path or road),
Stein (stone), *Turm* (tower), *Kopf* or *Kupp* (hilltop or summit),
Sonne (sun or sunny), *Lay* (slate rock), *Fels* (cliff), *Stück* (piece
of land), *Morgen* (rough equivalent of an acre), *Feld* or *Acker*
(field or acre), *Abt* (abbot), *Graf* (count), *Bischof* (bishop), *Herren*
(lords), etc. Keeping in mind that *alt* or *alten* means old, and *neu,*
new, that *nieder* and *unter* mean lower, and *ober,* upper, that *lange*
is long and *hohe* is high, that *schwarz* is black, *weiss,* white, *rot,* red,
and *gold,* gold, it is possible to make sense out of at least a majority
of German vineyard names. Here are a dozen examples:

Geisenheimer Altbaum	—from the "Old Tree" vineyard of Geisenheim
Piesporter Gräfenberg	—from the "Count's Hill" in Piesport
Deidesheimer Hohenmorgen	—from the "high Acres" of Deidesheim
Forster Kirchenstück	—from the "Church Section" of Forst
Deidesheimer Langenstück	—from "Long Section" of Deidesheim
Erbacher Markobrunn	—from the "Mark (or border) Fountain" vineyard of Erbach
Neumagener Rosengärtchen	—from the "Little Rose Garden" of Neumagen
Rüdesheimer Berg Rottland	—from the "Red Soil Hill" of Rüdesheim
Uerziger Schwarzlay	—from the "Black Slate" vineyard of Uerzig
Zeltinger Schlossberg	—from the "Castle Hill" of Zeltingen
Eltviller Sonnenberg	—from the "Sunny Hill" of Eltville
Kueser Weissenstein	—from the "White Stone" vineyard of Kues

2. German labels also tell you, in a majority of cases, in what year the wine was made. All good German wines carry a vintage, and it is fairly safe to bet that any wine that does not is ashamed of the year of its birth. But it is important to remember that all but the very best German wines mature early—only the true elite among the 1959s are still improving and the lesser wines, even of that incomparable vintage, are growing old.

3. If you understand their special terminology, German wine labels tell you whether or not a wine has been "chaptalized," or "sugared" (rather euphemistically, the Germans call such wines *verbesserte,* or improved). All *natural* wines carry one or more of the following designations on their labels, whereas no "improved" wine legally may do so:

Original-abfüllung
(estate-bottling)
Wachstum (growth)
Creszenz (growth)
Gewächs (growth)
Kellerabfüllung (cellar-bottled)
Kellerabzug (cellar-bottling)
Schlossabzug (castle-bottling)
Cabinet or *Kabinett* (cabinet wine)

Natur (natural)
Rein (clean, or genuine)
Ungezuckerter (unsugared)
Naturrein (natural and genuine)
Echt (genuine)
Fass No. (Cask Number)
Fuder No. (Cask number)
Edel (noble)
Spätlese (late picked)
Auslese (selection)
Beerenauslese (see Chapter I)
Trockenbeerenauslese (see Chapter I)

A rather more complete definition of most of these terms will be found in the glossary at the end of this chapter, but it may be useful to add that, more often than not, these words are joined and combined, after the German fashion, on a wine label. Thus you will find *Edelgewachs, Originalgewachs, Edelbeerenauslese,* and heaven knows how many more, all having their shades of meaning, but all carrying the definite assurance that the wines they describe have been made without the benefit of added sugar.

4. Especially when it comes to finer wines, German wine labels should give you specific information about the maturity of the grapes from which the wine was made. A given vineyard in a given year will produce a whole family of different wines, some of them worth ten times as much per bottle or per cask, as others. Forgetting those that have been sugared, or "improved," the gradations of Rüdesheimer Schlossberg, for example, are as follows:

Rüdesheimer Schlossberg (a fairly dry wine made from normally ripe grapes).

Rüdesheimer Schlossberg Kabinett (a wine of superior grade, which has been sold for a higher price—generally a fixed minimum price per barrel).

Rüdesheimer Schlossberg Spätlese (somewhat finer, a little less dry, worth perhaps 30% to 50% more than the first, and probably more than the second. Could also be called Kabinett).

Rüdesheimer Schlossberg Auslese (much fuller bodied, somewhat sweet, made from grapes specially selected during the harvest, worth at least twice as much as wine simply called Rüdesheimer Schlossberg; also entitled to the Kabinett designation).

Rüdesheimer Schlossberg Beerenauslese, or Trockenbeerenauslese (these are great rarities, produced in extremely limited quantities, essentially dessert wines, very sweet, very expensive; they can also be called Kabinett).

There exist other and more complicated sub-categories, and although these are listed and defined in the Glossary (page 28), perhaps a few words about them will not come amiss at this point.

First, the word *Kabinett* (or *Cabinet* or *Kabinettwein*). Originally wines so marked constituted a sort of private reserve of the vineyard owner, and in some cases were not offered for general public sale. The term originated in the Rheingau, and purists insist that properly it should not be used on any except Rheingau wines. To my knowledge, it has never been used in the Pfalz, rarely in Hessia (although frequently on the Nahe), and by only one or two major producers of the Moselle, and then only on bottles destined for export. Legally, the term has no standing and may be given by any producer to any wines he sees fit; in practice, however, among the great vineyard-owners of the Rhine, it has a very precise meaning, albeit one which varies from one vineyard-owner to another. At the State Domain (Steinberg, etc.) as at Schloss Vollrads and Schloss Reinhartshausen, *Kabinett* wines are all those that sell for over a certain fixed price per cask; this minimum varies considerably from one producer to another, and even occasionally from year to year. At Schloss Johannisberg the system is quite different, and a fuller explanation will be found in Chapter IV. Briefly and in general, a *Kabinett* wine is a superior grade, though certainly not a rarity—all *Auslesen,* and almost always all *Spätlesen,* have *Kabinett* rank, and in years such as 1953 so do many other wines of less distinguished origin but superior quality.

Second, particularly on the Moselle but also in Hessia, and on the Nahe, it is common and proper practice to distinguish between the various casks of *Spätlese* and *Auslese* which a given vineyard may produce in a good or great year by the words *feine* (fine), *feinste* (finest) and even *hochfeinste* (high-finest). These terms mean what they say, and a producer's *Hochfeinste Auslese* may be worth twice as much, and bring twice as much at auction, as his *Auslese.* To the true expert and wine-lover, Moselles of this sort are definitely to be preferred to the *Beerenauslesen* and *Trockenbeerenauslesen* which lose their "Mosel character" as they gain in sweetness, but of course the latter, being even more extraordinary rarities, bring an even higher price.

Third, it sometimes happens that a producer, in a great year, will come up with one cask that is altogether extraordinary. To this he may give the title of *Bestes Fuder* or *Bestes Fass*. This is as far as he can go, for it means that he has no better.

5. German wine labels quite often tell you (although sometimes indirectly and sometimes even by omission) the variety of grape out of which the wine was made. When a variety is mentioned, it is generally the best, the Riesling, and *it is fairly safe to assume that any wine from the Palatinate (Pfalz) or from Hessia or from Franconia (the Steinwein Country) which is not specifically labeled "Riesling" was made from another grape, in almost all instances the Sylvaner.* This rule holds true even for Liebfraumilch.

On the other hand, along the Moselle and in the Rheingau, the Riesling predominates to such an extent that the opposite is the case, and *a wine that carries no grape name may be presumed to be a Riesling.* The word "Riesling" on Moselle and Rheingau labels is therefore largely superfluous, although it is sometimes used. It should never be confused with and cannot replace a vineyard name—a Zeltinger Riesling is generally a blend of Riesling wines from the less distinguished parts of Zeltingen; a Zeltinger Schlossberg Riesling is an entirely different matter, for it comes from a great vineyard and it too is assuredly a Riesling whether or not it is so labeled.

It may be added that wines made, particularly in the Pfalz and in Baden, from an unusual grape variety such as Gewürztraminer are almost invariably so labeled.

6. Especially when it comes to the finer, the unsweetened and unblended wines, German labels are exceedingly specific as to the producer's name and guarantee. On other wines the shipper's name constitutes what might be called a brand, and a single house may own and use a dozen, or even fifty of them. Many admirable wines are shipped under such labels, or brands, just as there are many fine wines from the Bordeaux region of France which do not carry the mark and guarantee of chateau-bottling. Nevertheless, the consumer, in the long run, will do far better to give his confidence and his preference to German wines estate-bottled by the producer, for he is thus protected, not by the commercial standards of some export

house, but by the strict and rigidly-enforced controls of the German Government.

A German wine-producer's name is not in any sense a brand—it is the name of an individual who owns a certain specific vineyard, or vineyards, who makes his own wine and bottles it in his own cellar, who buys no wine from other producers, makes no blends, except possibly of two or more casks from the same parcel of his own vines, who generally does no advertising and has no sales department. He is the German equivalent of the owner of a Bordeaux chateau, or an estate-bottler in Burgundy, in France. In many cases he is a member of an association called the *Verband Deutscher Naturwein-Versteigerer* (literally, the association of German-natural-wine-auction-sellers). The seal of this group, which is a rather odd-looking eagle, of which the body is formed by a bunch of grapes, appears along the left-hand margin of many German wine labels, and there is no better mark of authenticity; wines from these producers are for the most part sold at auction, in barrels, with the explicit provision that they be bottled by the producer, when the producer sees fit, and delivered to the purchaser with the producer's label and branded cork. Such wines are never falsified; they may be magnificent or good or only fair, but they are unquestionably genuine.

It is perhaps unfortunate that German producers have not adopted some single phrase, easily recognizable by the consumer, to designate wines that are estate-bottled. By all odds the most common, however, is *Original-Abfüllung* (the abbreviation, often used, is Orig.-Abfg.), but *Keller-Abfüllung, Kellerabzug* and *Schlossabzug* mean virtually the same thing and can no less be relied upon.

Three other words, invariably used in direct conjunction with the producer's name, are also useful indications of authenticity, although they do not necessarily mean that a wine is estate-bottled. *Wachstum* and *Gewächs* (both terms originally come from the same Anglo-Saxon stem as the verb wax, and both mean "growth") are sure evidence that the wine is the unblended produce of a single named grower, and that it is natural, rather than sugared, or "improved." The French equivalent is a Bordeaux wine that carries the chateau label, but not the indications of chateau-bottling—it has been, or may have been, bottled elsewhere, in other words not by the grower, and quite often for wholly legitimate and proper reasons. These three words are therefore a good deal less specific than *Original-Abfüllung* and *Kellerabzug,* but you will hardly ever see them except on bottles that are quite genuine and altogether worthy. These terms, too, have their various complex and combined forms, and you will see *Eigenes Wachstum* (a bottler's own growth), *Edelgewächs* (noble growth), and many others. The one real essential is the producer's name, plus the clear and unequivocal statement that the name is that of a *producer,* not just a trade name, or brand.

It seems hardly necessary to add that over a period of years or decades or even centuries certain estates and certain families have acquired a reputation for the excellence of their wines which they have laboriously earned and scrupulously kept intact, and which they fully merit. The names of these members of what might be called the elite have been listed in the following chapters in connection with the villages where their vineyards lie. Their labels are known to every lover of German wines, and their names are regarded with deference and affection by all those, in whatever country, who respect craftsmanship and honesty and fine wine.

The following alphabetical list should prove useful for reference:

Terms frequently used on German wine labels, other than the name of the wine, and the vintage.

Abfüllung	Bottling. Kellerabfüllung, for example, means "bottled in the cellar of . . ."
Auslese	Literally, selection. A wine made from selected grapes, richer, sweeter, more expensive than others of the same year and vineyard.
Beerenauslese	Literally and actually means that the ripest grapes have been set aside, grape by grape, at vintage time, and a separate wine (this) made from them. A sweet, very expensive wine.
Bestes Fass (Fuder)	A producer's best wine of a given year.
Creszenz (Kreszenz)	Growth. Followed by a producer's (grower's) name means the wine is natural, unsugared.
Domane	Domain, or vineyard property or properties.

Echt	Genuine, authentic. Can only be used on unsugared wines.
Edel-	Noble. Used in conjunction with terms like Beerenauslese to indicate remarkable quality.
Eigengewächs	One's own production, or growth.
Erben	Heirs.
Fass No. . . .	Cask Number . . . May only be used on unsugared wines from the Rhine.
Feine (Feinste)	Fine (finest). Used on the Moselle with the terms Spätlese and Auslese to indicate an exceptionally good cask or lot.
Freiherr	Baron.
Fuder No. . . .	Cask Number . . . May only be used on unsugared wines from the Moselle.
Fürst	Prince.
Gebruder	Brothers. Gebruder Schmidt means Schmidt Brothers.
Geschwister	Brothers and sisters. Geschwister (or Geschw.) Berres means Brothers and Sisters of the Berres family.
Gewächs	Growth. Followed by a producer's (grower's) name means the wine is natural, unsugared.
Graf	Count.
Hoch-	High. Used in conjunction with terms like Beerenauslese to indicate very high quality.
Kabinett (Cabinet)	A wine of superior grade. See pages 25 and 78.
Keller	Cellar.
Kellerei	Cellars, or winery.

Naturrein	Made without the addition of sugar.
Naturwein	A natural wine, unsugared.
Original-Abfüllung (Orig.-Abfg.)	Bottled by the grower, estate-bottled.
Pfarrgut	Vineyard forming part of the endowment of the local clergy.
Rentamt	Revenue Office.
'sche	The equivalent of *'s* in English.
Schlossabzug	Bottled at the castle. See also Chapter IV.
Spätlese	Late-picking. A superior, natural wine made from grapes picked late in the season.
Spitzen-	Peak. Used in conjunction with terms like Beerenauslese to indicate top quality.
Stiftung	A charitable foundation, and its endowment.
Trockenbeerenauslese	A step above Beerenauslese. The individually picked grapes have been so ripe and sweet as to be practically dry ("trocken") or raisined. Such grapes give infinitesimal quantities of very sweet, wholly remarkable, and fabulously expensive wine.
Verwaltung (Gutsverwaltung)	Administration, or central office.
Wachstum	Growth. Followed by a producer's (grower's) name means the wine is natural, unsugared.
Weingut	Vineyard property, or domain. Its use on a label is *not* a guarantee of estate-bottling.
Winzergenossenschaft	A cooperative association of grape-growers which has set up a winery, cellar, and which sometimes bottles.
Winzerverein	A producers' cooperative, generally made up of smaller growers than the members of a Winzergenossenschaft.

III

MOSELLE

(Mosel-Saar-Ruwer)

AS far as their wines, as well as their waters, are concerned, the Moselle and its little tributaries, the Saar and the Ruwer, make up a single *Gebiet,* or basin, or district. It is true that a person (and not necessarily an expert) who tastes them comparatively can usually detect in the wines of the Saar a certain austerity and "hardness" which is their special charm, and which the Moselles as a whole do not possess. Similarly, the delicate, light, eminently gracious wines of the Ruwer have their unique qualities, and they, too, have their partisans. But all three are made entirely, almost invariably, from the Riesling grape, and all three have the same essential characteristics—an astonishing fragrant floweriness of bouquet, a fine remarkable cleanness on the palate, a refreshing lightness, for they hardly ever exceed 10-11% of alcohol by volume and are by far the lightest of the great wines of the world.

The Moselle River rises in the Vosges Mountains of France, and on its way to join the Rhine at Coblenz skirts both the Territory of the Saar and the Grand Duchy of Luxembourg. It enters Germany at the border town of Wasserbillig, which literally means "Cheap-water"—(and what wonder that water should be cheap in a country where the wine is so good!)

There do exist, therefore, a few Moselle wines which are not

German—the locally popular *vin gris* (a pale, rather acid, generally undistinguished *vin rosé*) produced round the old fortress city of Metz, in French Lorraine; and a whole collection of white wines produced in Luxembourg, most of which are pleasant, early-maturing, fun to drink on a summer afternoon, but of not much authority or consequence.

All of the great Moselles are German wines, and apart from those of the Saar and Ruwer, all of them come from one particular section of the Moselle Valley, known as the Mittel-Mosel.

Like all wine-growing districts, the Moselle has its share of wines which legally and technically are entitled to the name but are a long way from being a credit to it. A good many of these, especially in bad years, have had the full authorized maximum of 33⅓% of sugar and water added to them before fermentation, and plenty of the others, to the trained palate, have the unmistakable scent of heavy sulphur, which is perfectly harmless but usually the distinguishing mark of a wine whose sweetness is not altogether natural.

On the other hand, Moselle wines that carry the name of the actual vineyard, plus the *Original-Abfüllung* of a producer, are almost always irreproachable—the cheaper of them may possibly be a little tart, but all of them are well made and honest and sound. The good producers have their own high standards and they are not likely to ship, under the label of their estate and with their branded cork, a wine of which they are ashamed. The slightly higher price which such wines command (the difference often amounting to only a few pennies a bottle) is more than justified.

In a few of the better-known villages, such as Zeltingen and Piesport, there are a number of intelligent small growers—usually referred to as *Winzer* or *Bauern*—who are attempting to create a business for themselves, and a future for their children, by bottling their own wines. Such wines are generally very good and generally inexpensive—and such producers merit both the consumer's confidence and his help.

Apart from these, there are perhaps twenty or thirty "great" producers of established reputation. The names of the members of this aristocracy are set down in the following pages, in connection with the villages where their holdings lie. But a list of them is interesting all the same, for it constitutes a sort of special index to the small, complicated world of the Moselle Valley.

This is a rather feudal little world, easy-going, conservative, devoutly Catholic. Probably not one citizen of Trier in five ever read

MOSEL-SAAR-RUWER

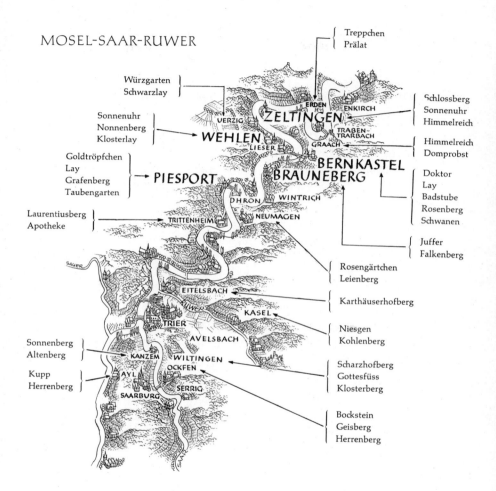

Treppchen
Prälat

Würzgarten
Schwarzlay

Sonnenuhr
Nonnenberg
Klosterlay

Goldtröpfchen
Lay
Grafenberg
Taubengarten

Laurentiusberg
Apotheke

Schlossberg
Sonnenuhr
Himmelreich

Himmelreich
Domprobst

Doktor
Lay
Badstube
Rosenberg
Schwanen

Juffer
Falkenberg

Rosengärtchen
Leienberg

Karthäuserhofberg

Niesgen
Kohlenberg

Sonnenberg
Altenberg

Kupp
Herrenberg

Scharzhofberg
Gottesfüss
Klosterberg

Bockstein
Geisberg
Herrenberg

ERDEN ENKIRCH
ZELTINGEN
UERZIG
TRABEN-TRARBACH
WEHLEN GRAACH
LIESER
BERNKASTEL
BRAUNEBERG
PIESPORT
DHRON WINTRICH
TRITTENHEIM NEUMAGEN
SAUER
EITELSBACH
KASEL
TRIER
AVELSBACH
KANZEM WILTINGEN
AYL OCKFEN
SERRIG
SAARBURG

a line written by Karl Marx, or is even aware that he was born and went to school there. As a matter of fact, the endowment of the school that Marx attended (the Friedrich Wilhelm Gymnasium) includes important vineyards, and you will see its name on wine labels.

Here are the great producers:

Staatsweingut (the German Government). Very large holdings, although not many of them of first rank, around Trier and in the Saar Valley—Avelsbach, Ockfen, Serrig.

Hohe Domkirche (the Cathedral of Trier). A few admirable vineyards, especially in the Scharzhofberg of Wiltingen, and in Avelsbach. The wines are sold as Dom Scharzhofberger and Dom Avelsbacher. 32 acres in all.

Bischöfliches Priesterseminar (a Catholic Seminary). Major estates amounting to 67 acres and producing an average of about 200 Fuder, roughly 20,000 cases a year, in Ayl, Kanzem and Wiltingen on the Saar, in Kasel on the Ruwer, and in Trittenheim, Dhron, Erden and Uerzig on the Moselle itself.

Bischöfliches Konvikt (a heavily endowed Catholic refectory for students). Good vineyards in Ayl on the Saar, in Eitelsbach and Kasel on the Ruwer, and in Piesport. 52 acres of vineyard.

Vereinigte Hospitien (a charitable foundation which, under the joint direction of the city of Trier and the Church, maintains a home for the aged and a hospital; the official list of its benefactors includes the name of Napoleon). Important holdings in Wiltingen, Kanzem and Serrig on the Saar, in Piesport on the Mittel-Mosel, and in the environs of Trier. 70 acres of vines.

Friedrich Wilhelm Gymnasium (a school). Next to the German State, the largest vineyard owner of all. Estates in Oberemmel and Ockfen on the Saar, in Trittenheim, Graach, Zeltingen, etc., but also in some of the less good townships such as Mehring.

St. Nikolaus Hospital (an ancient and famous hospital and home for the aged in Bernkastel-Kues). Excellent and important vineyards in Bernkastel, Graach, Lieser, Brauneberg, etc.

Kath. Pfarrkirche St. Michael (the endowment of a church in Bernkastel). Major holdings in Bernkastel and Graach.

Graf von Kesselstatt. Oberemmel, Niedermen-
nig, Wiltingen, Kasel, Piesport, Josephshof. ⎱ Old
⎰ Titled
Freiherr von Schorlemer. Lieser, Wintrich, Families
Brauneberg, Zeltingen, Graach. ⎰

Egon Müller. Scharzhof-Wiltingen. 16 acres.

Apollinar Joseph Koch. Wiltingen. 19 acres.

Von Hövel. Wiltingen. Oberemmel. 27 acres. Large
Landowners
Gebert. Ockfen. 25 acres. on the
Saar
Rheinart. Ockfen. 33 acres.

Lintz. Wawern. 17 acres.

Van Wolxem. Oberemmel. 15 acres.

Von Schubert. Maximin-Grünhaus. Large
Landowners
Rautenstrauch Erben. Eitelsbach. 37 acres. on the Ruwer

Patheiger. Kasel. 12 acres.

Thanisch. Bernkastel, Graach. 12 acres.

Joh. Jos. Prüm. Wehlen, Zeltingen, Bernkastel,
Graach. 12 acres.

Seb. Al. Prüm. Wehlen, Graach. 8 acres. Large
Landowners
Peter Prüm. Wehlen, Graach. 10 acres. on the
Mittel-
Zach. Bergweiler-Prüm Erben. (the heirs of Z. Mosel
Bergweiler-Prüm: cousins owning vineyards in
Brauneberg—*Licht-Bergweiler;* in Graach,
Bernkastel and Wehlen—*Adams-Bergweiler*
and *Pauly-Bergweiler*).

Large
Landowners
Thaprich. Bernkastel. on the
Mittel-
Christoffel. Erden. Uerzig. Mosel

Dr. Melsheimer. Traben-Trarbach, Bernkastel.

This list is of necessity so incomplete that I feel a little apolo-
getic about presenting it. Additional names have been included in the
descriptions of the wine-producing villages farther on in this chapter,
but no such list, unless it is to be of absurd proportions, can include
all the deserving, nor pretend to draw a sharp line between the

"great" and the near great. Those above are the names that appear on most of the distinguished wine lists in Germany and those that we may expect to find on the labels of the estate-bottled Moselles that we buy. But there are many smaller producers, and they should not by any means be disprized.

The little vineyard towns of the Saar and the Ruwer and the Mittel-Mosel are strung along their respective rivers like a string of beads. The high, green vine-covered slopes which have made their fame are divided into dozens of little plots or *Lagen,* each one with its special name, often shared by five or six or even more producers. In most cases there is no visible line, certainly no wall or natural boundary, which separates one *Lage* from another, but the growers know very well where one begins and the other ends, and the lines on the whole are scrupulously respected. All of the really outstanding vineyards have been listed in the following pages, under the heading of the village to which they belong.

It would be hard to write anything in the way of a paragraph or two which would do justice to the Moselle's unique beauty and its charm. The Moselle's best publicity agents are those that travel, in bottle, the world over, and perhaps the highest compliment that one can pay is to say that the country is as lovely as its wines.

THE MITTEL-MOSEL

The Mittel-Mosel is one of those terms that are almost meaningless and yet mean a great deal: the "Central Moselle," after all, has no official beginning and no legal end. To the geographer, it would certainly include all or most of that amazing serpentine valley—almost a gorge or a canyon—through which the Moselle runs between Trier and Bullay; but some authorities have given as its starting point the mouth of the tributary Saar, west and upstream from Trier, and others the frontier of the Grand Duchy of Luxembourg, even farther west.

This little book does not pretend to be a geography. It is a book about wine, and with a bow of apology to geologists and other learned folk, I have preferred to define the Mittel-Mosel in terms of its vineyards and its wine. Wine, after all, is the Valley's life and its livelihood; with one or two wholly minor exceptions, *all* of the really great wines produced on the banks of the Moselle come from its central section. Arbitrarily, then, for us, the Mittel-Mosel is the Moselle's district of great wines, it being understood that the equally great wines of the tributary Saar and Ruwer are to be considered separately and apart.

The Mittel-Mosel thus begins about ten Roman miles northeast of Trier—I say "Roman miles" since perhaps the best starting point is Mehring, and Mehring is just next door to the little village of Detzem, which takes its name from what was once the tenth milestone (*ad decimum lapidem*) on the old Roman road from Trier to Mainz. It ends at Enkirch, the last of some thirty villages which produce outstanding wine, a dozen or more out of the thirty being internationally famous. It is certainly one of the most interesting, as it is one of the most spectacularly beautiful, of all the wine-producing districts of the world.

See note 3-1

Mehring is only about fifteen miles from Enkirch as the crow flies. And yet by road or by railway or by shallow-draft river steamer the two are almost forty miles apart. There is no short-cut and no easy way round. No reluctant country schoolboy ever took so devious a route on his way to school as the Moselle on its way to join the Rhine at Coblenz, and perforce the road and the railway follow the river, since the steep valley walls are often six hundred to a thousand feet high. The river winds in loops and hairpin turns—its general direction is northeast, but the water is often running due southwest, or northwest or southeast, for that matter. About half of the slopes— never more—are covered with vineyards. All of these face more or less south—west-south-west to east-south-east being the extreme limits. They are extraordinarily steep, so steep that not ten percent of them can be worked by horse, let alone by tractor. Every corner and every shelf, be it under a cliff or on top of a cliff, that faces south or can be made to face south by skillful grading, has its quota of vines.

The reason is very simple. At this northern latitude grapes will only ripen with a more-or-less southern exposure, and they will only produce fine wine if they face practically due south, and are protected from the cold winds that blow, as late as May and as early as September, off the cold uplands of the Hunsrück and the Eifel.[1]

The soil, on the whole, is almost as forbidding as the climate. The hills are mostly slate, and slate for roofing can often be mined in the vineyards themselves. Virtually nothing will grow on this soil except the vine, and among vines only the Riesling does well—delicate, shy-bearing, late-maturing, hard to cultivate. Fortunately, it is

---

[1] "The grapevine," says a German proverb, "is a child of the sun; it loves the hills and hates the wind." *"Die Rebe ist ein Sonnenkind, sie liebt den Berg und hasst den Wind."*

one of the two best white wine grapes in the world, the Chardonnay or Pinot Chardonnay of Burgundy and Champagne being the other.

The labor is hand labor and there is no end to it. Every vine has its stake, an eight-foot sturdy support of peeled pine, and there are generally well over three thousand to the acre, all carried up from the road at the foot of the vineyard on the backs of men, like the manure which the vines must have in order to live, and the chips of slate, spread under the vines to hold the sun's warmth in autumn. These are annually washed down by the winter's rains, and annually replaced in the spring. At the vintage season, the grapes are brought down to the road in the same fashion, in great cone-shaped hods, but all year long the traffic is in the other and more difficult direction—tanks of copper sulphate spray (which gives an extraordinary almost sea-green color to the vine leaves in late summer), stakes, slate-chips, new vines for replanting, cord to tie the vines.

A good deal of this enormous yearly load goes up four or five hundred feet, by paths so steep that they are often quite literally stairways. With perhaps the single exception of the vineyards of the Vaudois, on the northern shore of Lake Geneva east of Lausanne, there are surely no wines on earth which require such an unconscionable amount of human labor per ton of grapes, or per bottle of wine. Nevertheless, you will go a long way before you find happier people, or people who take a greater pride in what they do, than those who cultivate their vines and make their pale, delicate, wonderful wine along the Mittel-Mosel. There are vintage festivals in almost every village in the fall; the villages are clean and the cellars immaculate, and the *Winzer* are a long, long way from being sorry for themselves. Like most people having to do with wine, they are extremely hospitable, and few things seem to give them greater pleasure than a compliment paid to their wine by a discriminating stranger.

The countryside, along the whole length of the river, is remarkably beautiful, and its air is one of quiet and pervading peace. Nothing on the Mittel-Mosel ever seems quite as important as the quality of the current year's vintage and perhaps, in the long run, nothing is.

By car, the trip from Detzem to Enkirch, which can be made in anywhere from an hour to a week, is one of the most memorable in Germany. By rail, on the antiquated little *Moseltalbahn,* which used to be called the *"Saufbähnchen"* or "drunkards' line" and may, for all I know, still deserve the name, it is perhaps less interesting, but nevertheless worthwhile. Certainly few wine-producing countries have the same combination of picturesqueness and color and great wine.

See note 3-1

Here, beginning with Mehring, is a roster of the wine-producing villages, of their vineyards and their wines:

Mehring. Hardly should be classified as part of the Mittel-Mosel. Its thin, short-lived little wines have much more in common with those of the villages of the Upper-Moselle (Schweich, Longuich, etc.) than with the great aristocrats of Piesport, Bernkastel and Wehlen. The *Friedrich Wilhelm Gymnasium* is the leading producer and the Zellerberg is regarded as the best vineyard. *Some 165 acres of vineyard, not 100% Rieslings.*

Detzem. More of a milestone than anything else. The best wines are only fair.

Thörnisch. *(About 75 acres of vineyard.)* Produces nothing of consequence except in the very greatest years. Thörnischer Enggass and Thörnischer Ritsch are its best-known vineyards and wines. *Adams, Ludes,* and *Zisch* are dependable producers.

Clüsserath. *(Some 220 acres under vines.)* Small wines, few of which are ever exported. Clüsserather Bruderschaft and Clüserrather Köningsberg are among the better *Lagen.*

Leiwen. *(200 acres.)* A small portion of Trittenheim's vine-covered hill lies within the communal limits of Leiwen, and a Leiwener Laurentiuslay of a great vintage can be a quite extraordinary wine.

* *Trittenheim.* *(About 225 acres.)* Caught in a hairpin loop of the river, its vineyards crowned with a picturesque little chapel dedicated to St. Lawrence (the Laurentiusberg), Trittenheim is the first major stone in the necklace of the Mittel-Mosel. Its extremely engaging and attractive little wines are fresh and light, early ready and not particularly long-lived. The *Bischöfliches Priesterseminar,* or Catholic Seminary of Trier, is the best-known bottler, but the *Friedrich Wilhelm Gymnasium, Josef Milz Jr., Dr. Ronde* and a few others are also worthy of confidence. The outstanding vineyards include:

Trittenheimer Laurentiusberg	Trittenheimer Apotheke
Trittenheimer Altärchen	Trittenheimer Clemensberg
Trittenheimer Sonnenberg	Trittenheimer Olk
Trittenheimer Falkenberg	Trittenheimer Neuberg
Trittenheimer Sonnteil	Trittenheimer Weierbach

* *Neumagen.*   *(Some 170 acres of vineyard.)* An interesting little
village, dating from Roman days and said to be the
oldest wine-producing town in Germany. Charming, secondary wines
not unlike those of Trittenheim, but in some instances with even more
bouquet. *Dünweg,* the *Willems'sche Armenstiftung, Dr. Ronde, Milz,
Schander,* and the *Pfarrkirche* are reliable producers.

Neumagener Rosengärtchen	Neumagener Leienberg
Neumagener Engelgrube	Neumagener Laudamusberg
Neumagener Kirchenstück	Neumagener Thierbach

* Dhron.   *(About 180 acres.)* Another sound and honorable *Weinberg,* although not one of the truly great ones; here again
you can count on the bottlings of the *Priesterseminar* and on those of
Dünweg, Dr. Ronde, Erz, Krebs and *Lehnert-Matheus.*

Dhronhofberger (or Dhroner	Dhroner Roterde
Hofberg)	Dhroner Kandel
Dhroner Grosswingert	Dhroner Hengelberg
Dhroner Sangerei	

*** *Piesport.*   *(Roughly 120 acres of vineyard.)* The tiny village of
Piesport consists of little more than two rows of
houses hemmed in between river and vineyard; back of it, and on both
sides, the high, precipitous hill that forms the north bank of the Moselle curves like the inside of a vast green bowl; its steep and rocky
face, looking due south, is covered with a mile-long expanse of unbroken vines. With such an exposure, Piesport could hardly fail to
produce fine wines, and there are many experts who will describe the
great Piesporters of great vintages as the Queens of the Moselle. Certainly there are few as good, for they are wonderfully delicate and
fragrant wines, never at all heavy, never at all coarse, with an incomparable distinction all their own. It must be admitted, however,
that a great deal of Piesporter (and even a great deal of Piesporter
Goldtröpfchen) is sold—far more, I suspect, than the 12,000 cases
which constitute the township's average annual production. In this
case, it is particularly important to insist on a specific vineyard name,
and to be sure that the labels carry the words *Original-Abfüllung,*
plus a producer's name. Among such producers are the *Vereinigte
Hospitien,* the *Bischöfliches Konvikt, Tobias,* the *Pfarrgut, Kesselstatt, Dünweg, Dr. Hain,* and a few smaller ones—*Haart, Bomberding,*

Lehnert, Weller, Reuscher and *Veit,* for example. Here are the most famous vineyards:

Piesporter Goldtröpfchen	Piesporter Lay
Piesporter Taubengarten	Piesporter Güntherslay
Piesporter Gräfenberg	Piesporter Falkenberg
Piesporter Treppchen	Piesporter Pichter
Piesporter Wehr	Piesporter Hohlweid
Piesporter Schubertslay	Piesporter Bildchen

Minheim. (100 acres.) Small wines, most of them usually sold in bulk, and perhaps some as Piesporter. Rosenberg is the best-known vineyard.

* *Wintrich. (About 200 acres.)* From a distance, the vineyards of Wintrich look like rocky stairways, with buttressed terrace walls holding up little green patches of vines. The wines have their full share of bouquet and breed, but are sometimes hard and lacking in charm except in great vintage years. *Von Schorlemer* is the best-known producer, but there are many good smaller ones. The top vineyards:

Wintricher Ohligsberg	Wintricher Geyerslay
Wintricher Sonnseite	Wintricher Neuberg
Wintricher Grosser Herrgott	Wintricher Rosenberg

* *Kesten. (Approximately 100 acres of largely mediocre vineyard.)* You are not likely to see the name Kestener on a wine list. One *Lage,* however, the Paulinshofberg, is justly famous; it belongs to *Franz Josef Liell* of Bernkastel; its wines are sold as Paulinshofberger, rather than as Kestener, and they bring high prices.

** *Brauneberg. (About 100 acres under vines.)* Until thirty or forty years ago this little hamlet was known as Dusemond (from the Latin *mons dulcis,* "sweet mountain"—supposedly so called because of the excellence and sweetness of its wines), and in the middle of the last century Brauneberger was the most celebrated and most highly prized of all the wines of the Moselle. But fashions change in wines as in so many other things, and Brauneberg today no longer rates in popularity with Piesport, Bernkastel and Wehlen. Its wines are nevertheless remarkable—with the Zeltingers, they are about the fullest-bodied of all Moselles, fine, rich wines of surprising authority and long life. The vineyard slope, the Brauneberg, or "brown hill," is almost as impressive as Piesport's, not curving but long, straight and high, and facing slightly east of south. There are many good producers—*Von Schorlemer, Ferdinand Haag*, the *St. Nikolaus Hospital, Licht-Bergweiler, Karp-Schreiber, Conrad, Kirch*, and the *Brauneberger Winzerverein* or Association of Wine Growers. Wines from the following *Lagen* command a premium:

Brauneberger Juffer	Brauneberger Falkenberg
Brauneberger Hasenlaufer	Brauneberger Kammer
Brauneberger Sonnenuhr	Brauneberger Lay

Mülheim.   (Some 120 acres.) Good secondary wines.

Veldenz.   (About 100 acres.) Not in the Moselle Valley proper but some two miles to the east, in a tributary valley, or *Seitental*. In good years, and in good years only, produces wines of remarkable freshness and bouquet that deserve to be better known than they are and that somewhat recall those of the Saar and the Ruwer. A Veldenzer Kirchberg of a good year is worth looking for.

* *Lieser.   (Some 240 acres of vineyard.)* Like most of the "near greats" of the Mittel-Mosel, Lieser has everything necessary to deserve top rank—except full southern exposure. The village consists of a few houses and an imposing 19th Century Schloss which belongs to the *Von Schorlemer* family, important wine-producers and bottlers. The *St. Nikolaus Hospital* of Bernkastel-Kues also has important holdings, and the two vineyards worthy of note (for wines from the others often have a pronounced *Bodenton,* or soil taste) are:

Lieserer Niederberg   Lieserer Schlossberg

*** *Bernkastel* (Bernkastel-Kues).   *(Some 450 acres under vines.)* This is about the most celebrated single name of the Moselle, though whether its wines on the whole are better than those of Piesport and Wehlen and Zeltingen is, I think, rather open to question. But few towns in Germany command such a magnificent view over river and vineyard, and few towns in the whole Moselle Valley are so quaint and charming; thanks to these advantages and to its excellent hotels and collection of picturesque little *Weinstuben,* or restaurants, both in Bernkastel and in Kues, directly across the river, its good road connections, and the well-known hospitality of its vintners, it has become a tourist center of considerable importance—the Rüdesheim, so to speak, of the Moselle. Meanwhile, of course, the fame of its Doktor vineyard has gone round the world.

Perhaps Bernkasteler Doktor's reputation (like that of many another wine) owes as much to the fact that the name is amusing and easy to remember as to the fact that the wine is good. The exceptional favor which it has long enjoyed in England dates, it is said, from a visit which Edward VII made to Bad Homburg, where he tasted the wine, liked it and ordered some "for home." But in the past few years it has become equally popular in America, and I rather suspect that over half the total production now crosses the Atlantic, where people still seem willing and able to pay the extraordinarily high price which it invariably commands, even in years of mediocre quality. Three producers (*Deinhard, Lauerburg* and *Thanisch*) own portions of the Doktor vineyard; of these, the late Dr. Thanisch was by all odds the most famous, and there is every reason to believe that his family will carry on his excellent and careful work. The Thanisch wine, invariably estate-bottled, is now sold as *Bernkasteler Doktor und Graben,* and in an average year less than 20,000 bottles go to market.

Since 1933, when I drank a bottle of Trockenbeerenauslese 1921 with Dr. Thanisch himself, I have tasted Bernkasteler Doktor, I suppose, two hundred times, so far without being able to detect the famous "smoky flavor" which some connoisseurs claim unerringly to perceive. Smoky or not, the wine does have a somewhat special taste, and is usually first rate. There are, however, other Moselles that I would class at least on a par with it, or above it, and several other vineyards in the town of Bernkastel deserve, it seems to me, almost equal rank. In addition to the *Thanisch* family (who have other vineyards as well as Doktor in Bernkastel, plus one or two in Graach), the top-rate producers include *Johann Josef Prüm, the Pfarrkirche St. Michael, Thaprich, Geller, Pauly-Bergweiler, Liell, Dr. Melsheimer,* and above all the *St. Nikolaus Hospital* of Kues, which is the village directly across the bridge from Bernkastel. The leading vineyards:

Bernkasteler Doktor	Bernkasteler Lay
(or Doktor und Graben)	Bernkasteler Schlossberg
Bernkasteler Badstube	Bernkasteler Pfalzgraben
Bernkasteler Rosenberg	Bernkasteler Schwanen
Bernkasteler Theurenkauf	Bernkasteler Steinkaul
Bernkasteler Bratenhöfchen	Bernkasteler Held

Bernkasteler Altenwald   Bernkasteler Pfaffenberg
Kueser Weissenstein

*** *Graach.* *(240 acres of vineyard.)* At Bernkastel the winding Moselle, running generally southwest to northeast, performs
a major convolution and sets out northwestward. Unlike the vineyards
of Trittenheim and Piesport and Brauneberg, which are on the left,
or north, bank of the river, those of Graach and Wehlen and even
Bernkastel are on the right, or south, bank. They overlook the river
and face south; this sounds illogical, and it most certainly is.

There is nothing strange or wrong, however, about the wines of
Graach—they are typical and lovely Mittel-Mosel vines, well-bal-
anced, fragrant and fine. It may be well to add that one Graacher wine
is not sold as Graacher—produced back of the Josephshof, which is
the property of the *Kesselstatt* family, it is marketed simply as
Josephshöfer. The other leading producers are *Thanisch, Johann
Josef Prüm, Von Schorlemer, Peter Prüm, S. A. Prüm Erben, Dr.
Weins Erben,* the *St. Nikolaus Hospital,* the *Pfarrkirche St. Michael,*
the *Friedrich Wilhelm Gymnasium, Kees-Kieren, Adams-Bergweiler,
Pauli-Combali* and *Pauly Bergweiler.* The best *Lagen:*

Graacher Himmelreich	Graacher Domprobst
Graacher Stablay	Graacher Abtsberg
Graacher Goldwingert	Graacher Münzlay
Graacher Lilienpfad	Graacher Mönch
Graacher Homberg	Graacher Heiligenhaus

*** *Wehlen.* *(Some 210 acres of vineyards.)* Fifty brief years ago,
Wehlen was considered by most experts to be nothing
more than a *Guter Weinort,* a village of good wines that ranked considerably below Graach and by no means in a class with Bernkastel
and Brauneberg. Today its best wines command higher prices even
than Bernkasteler Doktor, and most German *Feinschmecker* will tell
you that it is the best wine-producing village of the whole Mittel-
Mosel. This change is largely due to the efforts of a single family
called Prüm. What the DuPonts are to Delaware, the Prüms are, in
their own remarkable way, to Wehlen. Their big, comfortable, old-
fashioned stone houses stand one beside the other along the river,
and facing them, beyond the Moselle's only suspension bridge, are the
steep vineyards which have made the family fortune and its name.

In the center of these vineyards, between Graach and Zeltingen, a cliff has been cut away and painted to form an enormous white *Sonnenuhr,* or sundial. Year in and year out, for some three decades, the wines from Wehlen's Sonnenuhr vineyard have consistently brought the highest prices of any wines of the Moselle, and I think deservedly so. At their best, the Wehleners have no superiors and few equals—flowery, well balanced, with an almost supernatural combination of delicacy and richness, they are perfection itself.

Of course, this is by no means to say that all Wehleners are outstanding (for they are not) or consistently better than their neighbors, which is certainly doubtful. But the sign of Wehlen plus the name of Prüm on a wine label is what an astrologer would call a favorable combination, and it is usually the portent of something that will be well above the average when the cork is drawn.

The leading producers (mostly Prüms) are *Johann Josef Prüm, Sebastian Alois Prüm, Peter Prüm, Dr. Bergweiler* (collaterally a Prüm), *Dr. Weins Erben* (also a Prüm connection), *Hauth-Kerpen, Dietz, Weyer-Hauth* and the *St. Nikolaus Hospital.* The best vineyards:

Wehlener Sonnenuhr	Wehlener Nonnenberg
Wehlener Lay	Wehlener Rosenberg
Wehlener Klosterlay	Wehlener Abtei
Wehlener Feinter	Wehlener Wertspitz

* * * *Zeltingen.* *(About 470 acres of vineyards.)* This is a rather dull and quiet little town, dwarfed and overshadowed by the incredible steep expanse of five hundred acres of vineyard that rise behind it. Its production is the largest of any town on the Moselle, and certainly a vast amount of "Zeltinger" is made and sold which could hardly be described as distinguished even by the most charitable of critics. On the other hand, there is probably not a single village in the whole Moselle Valley which produces wines which on the average are as good as those of Zeltingen, and I am not sure that any village, including Wehlen, produces wines better than Zeltingen's best. To get the best, needless to say, you must ask not for "Zeltinger" but for the town name plus that of a better-than-average vineyard, and for an *Original-Abfüllung,* though the name of the bottler is less important here than in most other wine-producing towns. A good many of the *Bauern,* or small producers, bottle their own wines in Zeltingen, and these quite often have the double charm of being good and most reasonably priced.

Fairly full-bodied for a Moselle, the typical Zeltinger of a vineyard such as Himmelreich or Schlossberg has a combination of qualities which is truly extraordinary—softness, breed, bouquet and a charm which even those who are not Moselle-lovers will find hard to resist.

The "great" producers are some four or five in number—*Von Schorlemer, Johann Josef Prüm, Ehses-Berres, Ehses-Geller, Merrem,* and among the *Bauern,* or farmers, with small holdings in excellent vineyards, it would perhaps be well to note the numerous members of a family called *Ames* (pronounced ah-mes). The label of the *Frühmesse Stiftung* is another that can be counted on.

There are at least sixty or seventy officially recognized vineyards, or *Lagen,* on Zeltingen's great hill, and of these, here are the best:

Zeltinger Schlossberg	Zeltinger Sonnenuhr (or Sonnuhr)
Zeltinger Himmelreich	Zeltinger Rotlay
Zeltinger Steinmauer	Zeltinger Kirchenpfad
	Zeltinger Stephanslay

** *Erden.* *(Some 200 acres under vines.)* This is a poor and dull little village on the right bank of the river. Its superb steep vineyards (the best is called Treppchen,[2] or "little stairway," and this is an understatement) adjoin those of Uerzig, and can only be reached from Erden by boat. Many of the major vineyard owners, as might be expected, live elsewhere. Important producers include the *Bischöfliches Priesterseminar, Richard Josef Berres* and *Geschw, Berres, Christoffel Schmitges Erben, Schomann, Schwaab-Scherr, Orthmann-Matty.* The vineyards are as vertiginous as any on the Moselle, and one can only be astonished at the patience and determination of those who have created and who tend them. To open a bottle of a great Erdener of a year like 1949 or 1953 is to feel that perhaps the infinite and unending labor of the *Winzer* has not been wasted, for the wines in great years are wholly magnificent. Even in relatively poor years, I have tasted *Auslese* and *Beerenauslese* wines from Erden which were extraordinary. The best *Lagen:*

Erdener Treppchen	Erdener Prälat
Erdener Busslay	Erdener Hödlay

---

[2] Father Hennen, of the Bischöfliches Priesterseminar, tells me that the name Treppchen dates only from 1808 and that this vineyard was formerly called Unter-Uerzig. The change is certainly for the better.

Erdener Herrenberg   Erdener Kaufmannsberg
Erdener Filiusberg   Erdener Herzlay
      Erdener Kranklay

** *Uerzig.* *(About 110 acres.)* After Zeltingen, the Moselle abruptly changes direction once more, and resumes its normal and proper northeasterly course toward Coblenz. The vineyards of Uerzig, like those of Erden, which are just next door, are therefore on the left, or north, bank of the river. They are among the most spectacular of the whole Moselle Valley: most of them mere patches of green, carved out of the face of a cliff-like hill which is almost the color of brick. There is said to be a good deal of iron in the soil of Uerzig, and the wines, in any case, have a quality all their own. They mature rather slowly and require a good deal of special care and handling in the cellar before bottling; like the wines of the Saar they are often slightly *spritzig,* which means that they have an almost imperceptible tendency to be naturally sparkling; they are sharp and hard in poor years, but in good years they have an odd and wonderful spiciness and piquancy (the Germans call them *würzig* and *pikant*) which makes them, for an expert, among the easiest to recognize and place of all German wines. Unlike Zeltinger, Uerziger is by no means a name to look for on less expensive bottles, but an Uerziger Würzgarten of a great vintage, particularly if it is a *Spätlese* or an *Auslese,* can hold its own against the best, and can be one of the greatest wines of Germany. Outstanding producers include *Richard Josef Berres, Geschw. Berres, Eymael,* the *Bischöfliches Priesterseminar* and *Christoffel Erben.* Here are the best vineyards:

Uerziger Würzgarten   Uerziger Schwarzlay
Uerziger Lay   Uerziger Kranklay

Kinheim. *(About 200 acres.)* Wines of no great distinction and quality. The best vineyards are Kinheimer Rosenberg, Kinheimer Löwenberg and Kinheimer Hubertuslay. *Niedhöfer* is a reputable producer.

Cröv (or Kröv). *(Some 260 acres.)* Another mediocre vineyard town, although a very ancient and a very pretty one. Like Zell, of which more later, it has acquired a certain rather doubtful fame on account of an unusual and comic wine label. The label in question reads Cröver (sometimes Kröver) Nacktarsch, or "naked bottom," and shows a boy being spanked, with his pants down. The wines of Cröv are better than the label, and needless to say, Nacktarsch is not a vineyard. The best *Lagen* (their wines are often shipped as "Nacktarsch") include the following:

Cröver Niederberg   Cröver Heislay
Cröver Stephansberg   Cröver Petersberg

* *Traben-Trarbach.* *(Over 400 acres of vineyard.)* In reality, two villages, as the name would indicate—Traben on the left bank of the Moselle, and Trarbach on the right. Both little towns are picturesque, and are important tourist centers; and both are important in the Moselle wine trade as well. In general, the wines of Traben are small, but fresh and agreeable and charming; those of Trarbach have a little more authority, and in particularly good years a fine bouquet and a certain real distinction. *Dr. Melsheimer* is a reliable producer, and the following vineyard names are worth noting:

Trarbacher Schlossberg   Trarbacher Ungsberg
Trarbacher Huhnersberg   Trarbacher Königsberg

Enkirch. *(Some 320 acres.)* Officially, Enkirch marks the end of the Mittel-Mosel, the district of great wines. For although there are vineyards along the slopes all the way down to Coblenz, the best of these hardly yield anything better than *Consum-Weine*—those fresh and fragrant little carafe wines that are drunk when less than a year old. There are a few exceptions, of which Valwig, Winningen and Zell are the most important; the first two produce some really excellent bottles in great years, and Zeller Schwarze Katz, with the familiar black cat on its label, is one of the most famous of all German wines, although a long way from one of the best. Enkirch, however, is another matter—its delicate wines are true products of the Mittel-Mosel, and I have tasted some that were genuinely outstanding. The better vineyards:

Enkircher Steffensberg   Enkircher Battereiberg
Enkircher Herrenberg   Enkircher Montenubel

THE SAAR

The Moselle's largest tributary, which hurries down to join it west of Trier, is the silvery, winding and shallow Saar. Here in Germany, hardly more than a stone's throw from the border of Luxembourg, this famous little river runs through a green and smiling countryside— all fresh meadows and fruit trees and wide expanses of steep hillside vineyards—and it looks like anything but what it is: the stream that drains the celebrated Saar Basin, which is one of the most important centers of heavy industry in Western Europe.

Here, the blast furnaces and rolling mills of the upper Saar seem a thousand miles away, and from picturesque Saarburg, with its ruined castle, all the way down to the rather dreary little town of Conz, where it meets the Moselle, the river runs past a succession of sleepy villages. On every slope that faces south, or nearly south, you can see the orderly green pattern of perfectly tended vines.

This whole district was nevertheless the scene of heavy fighting during the early spring of 1945. The anti-tank defenses, the so-called "dragon's teeth" of the Siegfried Line, ran through some of the best vineyards, and when I visited the Saar for the last time before the War, in the summer of 1939, pill-boxes were even being constructed in the gardens of my good friend, Herr Koch, of Wiltingen. I remember that I congratulated another friend, in Oberemmel, on the completion of a magnificent new barn, which looked most impressive from a distance; he winked and whispered to me that it was a very wonderful barn indeed, with "walls of concrete one and a half meters thick."

When I returned in 1946, the pill-boxes, like the "barn," had been destroyed, but the whole Saar Valley was still littered with the ugly debris of war. There were still brass cartridge cases in the grass along the roadsides, and there was still a fighter plane which had crashed and miraculously not burned, smack in the center of the Scharzhofberg vineyard. A good many of the villages had been damaged by shellfire, many of the vines overrun by tanks, and there were plenty of others that had been neglected and seemed lost beyond repair.

Fortunately, Nature, when aided by a good deal of hard work on the part of humans, has a way of covering and obliterating these scars. Today the Saar Valley looks very much as it did when I first visited its cellars over twenty years ago. Most of my old friends (or their sons) are at work in their reconstructed vineyards; the War is largely forgotten, and the best Saar wines are magnificent, just as they were when I first made their acquaintance in the 1930's.

These wines of the Saar, it may be well to point out, are not to everybody's taste. The Germans have a saying that "in poor years the *Saarwein* is a beggar and in good years a noble lord." To be more specific, they are even more subject than the other wines of the Moselle to the caprices of weather and season. The Saar Valley is a cold little land of late spring and frequent sudden frosts; even in mid-May and early October it has far more than its share of hailstorms and icy days. At least three years out of ten produce wines that have to be "sugared" and can only be used for the manufacture of *Sekt,* or sparkling wine. In two or three more years per decade, the wine is so hard and sharp (the Germans call it *stahlig,* or steely, and the adjective is well chosen) that only the local enthusiasts can tolerate it. Perhaps two other years out of ten yield wine that is sound and good but not extraordinary. But once, twice, or at most three times in a decade, nature is kind. And in such years the Saar produces a certain number of wines which are, to my palate, the noblest and most remarkable white wines in the world.

This, I realize, is not something one should say lightly. Wine experts, after the fashion of sailors, are supposed to have their loves in every country, and to promise undying fidelity to each one, impartially, every time they taste it. But with all due respect to Château d'Yquem and to Montrachet, to Marcobrunner and Imperial Tokay, I still say, give me a perfect Scharzhofberger (or a Wiltinger or an Ockfener) of a great year.

In these great and exceedingly rare wines of the Saar, there is a combination of qualities which I can perhaps best describe as indescribable—austerity coupled with delicacy and extreme finesse, an incomparable bouquet, a clean, very attractive hardness tempered by a wealth of fruit and flavor which is overwhelming—and all this in a wine which hardly exceeds 10% of alcohol by volume (whereas Montrachet and Yquem are rarely under 13% and frequently much higher). Let me say once more that only the greatest Saar wines deserve this sort of praise, that there is far more bad Saar wine than good, and that the best is never inexpensive. On the whole, the wines of the Mittel-Mosel are a much safer bet. But the Saar . . . is the Saar.

Here, as one goes up the Saar from its junction with the Moselle, are the principal wine-producing towns and their vineyards, with an idea of their acreage under vines:

Filzen. *(About 60 acres of vineyard.)* Undistinguished, except in the greatest years. *Piedmont Erben* is a dependable producer, and the best wines are:

Filzener Pulchen	Filzener Urbelt
Filzener Vogelberg	Filzener Karlberg

* *Wawern.* *(About 70 acres.)* On the west or left bank of the Saar. Good but not great. *Lintz* is a reputable and important (I might even say celebrated) vineyard owner, and *Le Gallais* another good name. The best vineyards:

Wawerner Herrenberg   Wawerner Goldberg

* *Kanzem* (or Canzem). *(Roughly 100 acres.)* The village is on the west side of the Saar, but the vineyards, across the narrow river, cover a great steep hillside and face south. The wines in good years are excellent, with a special spicy flavor and a great deal of charm. The leading producers include the *Vereinigte Hospitien,* the *Bischöfliches Priesterseminar, Weissebach Erben* and *H. J. Patheiger.*

Kanzemer Sonnenberg	Kanzemer Berg
Kanzemer Altenberg	Kanzemer Wolfsberg
Kanzemer Unterberg	Kanzemer Horecker
Kanzemer Kelterhaus	

*** *Wiltingen.* *(About 330 acres of vineyards.)* Ranks with Piesport, Bernkastel, Wehlen and Zeltingen as one of the incomparable best. Two of its wines are nevertheless so famous that they rarely carry the name of Wiltingen, but are sold instead as Scharzhofberger and Scharzberger. The Scharzhof itself is a lovely old manor house, which has been the property of the Müller family for generations. Three or four other vineyards in Wiltingen are quite in the class with the Scharzhofberg, and produce, like the Saar as a whole, wonderful wines in good years and wines of little or no interest in years of insufficient sunshine. The famous producers are *Egon Müller* (owner of the Scharzhof), *Apollinar Joseph Koch,* the *Hohe Domkirche* or Cathedral of Trier (producer of "Dom Scharzhofberger"), the *Vereinigte Hospitien,* the *Bischöfliches Priesterseminar,*

Van Volxem, Le Gallais, the Bischöfliches Konvikt, Kesselstatt, Graf zu Hoensbroech and Von Hövel. The best vineyards:

Scharzhofberg (or Wiltinger Scharzhofberg)

Wiltinger Braune Kupp	Wiltinger Gottesfüss
Wiltinger Rosenberg	Wiltinger Klosterberg
Scharzberg (or Wiltinger Scharzberg)	Wiltinger Braunfels
Wiltinger Dohr	Wiltinger Kupp

** Oberemmel. (Some 200 acres.) Just east of Wiltingen, includes part of Scharzberg. Another village which in great years produces wines which can only be described as extraordinary. Von Hövel and Kesselstatt are the most important vineyard owners. The good vineyards:

Oberemmeler Hütte	Oberemmeler Rosenberg
Oberemmeler Altenberg	Oberemmeler Agritiusberg
Oberemmeler Karlsberg	Oberemmeler Raul
Scharzberg (or Oberemmeler Scharzberg)	Oberemmeler Eltzerberg

* Niedermennig. (Roughly 90 acres.) Another good little vineyard town which deserves to be better known. Simon Erben and Kesselstatt are major producers. Note:

Niedermenniger Sonnenberg	Niedermenniger Herrenberg
Niedermenniger Euchariusberg	Niedermenniger Zuckerberg

** Ayl. (About 110 acres of vines.) This little village west of the Saar owes its fame to one magnificent hillside facing south and completely planted with vines. The Bischöfliches Konvikt and the Bischöfliches Priesterseminar are labels to look for, but there is also an important Winzerverein. The best Lagen include:

Ayler Kupp   Ayler Herrenberg
Ayler Neuberg

** Ockfen. (Some 200 acres.) Produces a few wines which, in years such as 1949 and 1953, are truly superb and among the best of the whole Saar Valley. The top producers are the State Domain (Staatsweingut), Adolf Rheinart Erben, Gebert, Geltz and

Max Keller, particularly the three first mentioned, and the great vineyards are few but outstanding:

Ockfener Bockstein	Ockfener Geisberg
Ockfener Herrenberg	Ockfener Heppenstein
Ockfener Oberherrenberg	

Saarburg. (About 100 acres.) The picturesque little center of the Saar wine trade, but more celebrated for its beauty than for its wines. A few vineyards are perhaps worth mentioning:

Saarburger Leyenkaul	Saarburger Schlossberg
Saarburger Mühlberg	Saarburger Rausch

Serrig. (Some 250 acres of vineyard.) As you go up the Saar Valley, the climate becomes increasingly unfavorable almost from one mile to another, and the vineyards are less and less dependable as far as quality is concerned. Wiltingen, for example, will make good wine perhaps two years out of five, but Saarburg and Serrig only about once a decade. A great Serriger of a great vintage (1937, 1949, 1953) is something quite remarkable—but I have tasted perhaps a dozen such, and at least two hundred poor ones. The *Staatsweingut* and the *Vereinigte Hospitien* are major producers. Heiligenborn, Hindenburgslei, Würzberg, Marienberg, Wingertscheck, Kupp and Schloss Saarfels are the most important vineyards.

THE RUWER AND THE DISTRICT OF TRIER

The venerable and colorful little city of Trier, which was to a large extent in ruins in 1945, has risen miraculously from its ashes, like all of Western Germany. Its daily market is bright with flowers again, its streets in summer are full of tourists, and the dining-room tables of its hotels are heavy with good food and slender green bottles of Moselle, just as they were twenty years ago. In the center of town stands Trier's most impressive relic of Roman days, the *Porta Nigra,* a three-story fortified gateway of dark stone, which survived the last war as it has survived other wars without number in the eighteen hundred years of its existence; northeast of the city a whole new district of small homes is under construction, and there is even a traffic circle, in the American style.

Some two or three miles beyond the traffic circle, on the road that leads downstream toward the vineyards of the Mittel-Mosel, the valley narrows and a little river tumbles down to join the Moselle out of the high, cold, pine-covered hills of the Hunsrück. This is the Ruwer (pronounced Roo-ver)—it looks a good deal more like a trout stream than like a river, but its wines are famous. The Ruwer (it has of course nothing to do with the Ruhr, which is northeast of Cologne) runs north, and since the vineyards face south, they are not visible until you start up the valley; then, off to the left and right of the winding road and the narrow stream, you see one wide steep hillside after another planted with vines. The soil, as on the Mittel-Mosel and the Saar, is largely slate, and the construction and cultivation of the vineyards require an amount of hand labor which is almost incredible.

Happily, at least in good years, the Ruwer wines are worth all this effort. Hard and even acid in years like 1944, 1951 and 1954, they have a wonderful lightness and an exquisite flowery fragrance when they are at their best, and I have tasted marvelous wines from Eitelsbach, and Grünhaus and Kasel which were well under 9% of alcohol by volume. This means that they are in general the lightest of all the fine wines of the world, and an obscure local poet has described them as a combination of "the fire of the sun, the gold of the stars and cool moonlight"—"*Sonnenfeuer, Sternengold, kühlen Mondlichtschein.*"

In the Ruwer Valley proper there are only three wine-producing villages of more than passing interest, and perhaps a half-dozen major producers in all. The town of Zeltingen alone produces as much as the whole Ruwer Valley. Here are the three villages:

** *Maximin Grünhaus.* (*Some 120 acres.*) The largest estate is that of the celebrated *Von Schubert* family, and their lovely old-fashioned label is a welcome and reassuring sight on a wine bottle. The vineyards are on the left, or west, bank of the Ruwer, and the wines are sold as *Maximin Grünhäuser,* plus in many cases the name of the specific *Lage* such as Herrenberg or Bruderberg.

** *Eitelsbach.* (*About 75 acres.*) Facing Maximin-Grünhaus across the valley, the ancient Carthusian Monastery of Eitelsbach has become Eitelsbacher Karthäuserhofberg, and when you add to this not inconsiderable mouthful a vineyard name, plus

Original-Abfüllung H.W. Rautenstrauch Erben (the owners) you get something very nearly unpronounceable by American standards. Here, too, the label is an unusual and an interesting one—a sort of elaborate little collar around the neck of the bottle—and there used to be a joke to the effect that the wine in Germany with the longest name had the smallest label. But the wine is admirable, delicate and well-balanced. Apart from *Rautenstrauch,* the *Bischöfliches Konvikt* of Trier is the principal producer, and the best vineyards include:

> Eitelsbacher Karthäuserhofberger Kronenberg
> Eitelsbacher Karthäuserhofberger Sang
> Eitelsbacher Karthäuserhofberger Burgberg
> Eitelsbacher Marienholz

* *Kasel* (or Casel). *(Some 240 acres.)* The largest and most important vineyard town of the *Ruwertal.* The Kaseler wines, while rarely great, are almost unfailingly pleasant, light and fresh and full of bouquet and charm. The *Bischöfliches Priesterseminar,* the *Bischöfliches Konvikt, Von Beulwitz* and *Kesselstatt* are major producers, and the best vineyards include the following:

Kaseler Niesgen	Kaseler Taubenberg
Kaseler Steiniger	Kaseler Kohlenberg
Kaseler Kernagel	Kaseler Hitzlay
Kaseler Herrenberg	Kaseler Höcht

Waldrach. Upstream and back of Kasel, the little town of Waldrach has one well-known estate, *Schloss Marienlay.*

THE DISTRICT OF TRIER

On the hills just south of Trier, halfway between the valley of the Ruwer and that of the Saar, there are a few vineyards, one of which is deservedly famous; five or six others, in good years, yield wines well above the average. Several of these wines, although by no means the best of them, are actually produced within the city limits of Trier itself, and one or two other rather better ones practically in the suburbs. Possibly worth noting is the so-called Tiergärtener of the *Weingut Von Nell* and the pleasant lesser wines of *Zeimet Erben,* of Olewig. The one vineyard of real consequence is:

* *Avelsbach.* *(Over 120 acres.)* As might be expected, the Avels-
bachers have all the faults as well as a good many of
the virtues of the wines of the Ruwer and the Saar. They are exceedingly hard and acid except in great vintage years; they have a superb
bouquet; they are very light, very pale, very fresh, rather tart; in a
fabulous year such as 1949 they are magnificent, but even in a great
year like 1953 the average consumer is likely to find some of them,
although of course not the Spätlesen and Auslesen, a little too steely
for his taste. The largest vineyard owners are the German Government
(*Staatsweingut*) and the Cathedral of Trier (*Hohe Domkirche*). The
Cathedral's wines are sold as "Dom-Avelsbacher." And the best
Lagen:

Avelsbacher Herrenberg	Avelsbacher Hammerstein
Avelsbacher Altenberg	Avelsbacher Rotlei

IV

RHEINGAU

O NCE it leaves the Swiss border at Basel, the Rhine runs almost due north toward Holland and the North Sea; it flows tranquilly but swiftly down that splendid and fertile valley, that vast flat trough which it has cut for itself between the Black Forest and the Alsatian Vosges; it passes within sight of the Haardt Mountains of the Palatinate on its left, and the wooded hills of Baden on its right; it skirts the red, terraced vineyards of Nierstein and Nackenheim and sweeps majestically on northward down to Mainz.

At Mainz this steady northerly progress ends abruptly, and the face of the river changes. Directly in its path rises the high, forest-covered barrier of the Taunus Hills; the Rhine broadens and curves west, and for twenty miles, from Mainz to Rüdesheim and Bingen, it flows, not north, nor even west, but actually south of west. And the lower slopes of these same Taunus Hills are one great vineyard. This is the Rheingau—the *Weingau,* as the Germans call it—and among the celebrated viticultural districts of the world, it has the Burgundian Côte d'Or for its only real rival.

Unlike Bordeaux, unlike Champagne, unlike the Moselle Valley even, this is not a whole wine-growing region—it is a single hillside, steeper to be sure in some places than in others, cut by its minor depressions and little valleys, but protected everywhere against the cold north wind by the wooded mass of the Taunus, and everywhere, or almost everywhere, facing due south over the river, so that its Rieslings get the full benefit of the southern sun.

There are other sections of this incomparable Rhine Valley which are perhaps more impressive than the Rheingau, but none, surely, more gracious and more beautiful. The quiet, shady terraces of its little vineyard towns overlook the river; they are fragrant in summer with linden blossoms—wonderfully inviting places to sit and relax over a good bottle or two. The Rhine, among other things, is one of the great commercial arteries of Western Europe, and the constant river traffic gives the whole scene a special liveliness and charm. There are barges and string of barges—French and sometimes Belgian, Swiss and Dutch and German; there are sailboats and excursion steamers, canoes and kayaks, and even rare occasional patrol-boats flying the American or the British flag. The narrow river road, the *Rheinstrasse,* is busy too—crowded all summer long with tourists, youngsters on bicycles, buses from every part of Western Germany and even from Scandinavia, cars with the license plates of a dozen different countries.

Behind all this bustle and activity, and wholly unaffected by it, but constituting the real life of the Rheingau, is the old and solid and sound tradition of good wine. In almost every one of the little river towns there are one or two old patrician families who, for generations, have owned their famous vineyards and made their famous wines, and whose labels are known from Chicago to Cape Town, and from Manila to Maine. Thus in Eltville there is Graf Eltz who, in addition to the superb Eltzerhof here on the Rhine, is the owner of Burg Eltz on the Moselle—perhaps the loveliest castle in all Germany. In Eltville, too, is the gracious, ancient home of the Von Simmern family; the old Baron, whom I knew before the war, spoke half a dozen languages and had been German Ambassador to Spain. In Erbach, and directly on the river, is Schloss Reinhartshausen, the celebrated estate of Prince Heinrich Friedrich of Prussia, a cousin of the last Kaiser. In Hallgarten there is the estate of Prince Löwenstein, and in Hattenheim that of Graf von Schönborn, one of whose ancestors signed, in nearby Geisenheim, the treaty ending the Thirty Years' War. Schloss Johannisberg, of course, has been owned by the Metternich family since 1816, and Graf Matuschka, of Schloss Vollrads, is President of the German Wine Growers Association. The Von Brentanos, of Winkel, were friends of Goethe, and the present Foreign Minister of Germany is one of their connections. In Rüdesheim and Kiedrich are the estates of Baron von Ritter zu Groenesteyn, and in Lorch there is Graf von Kanitz. These are only a few of the more

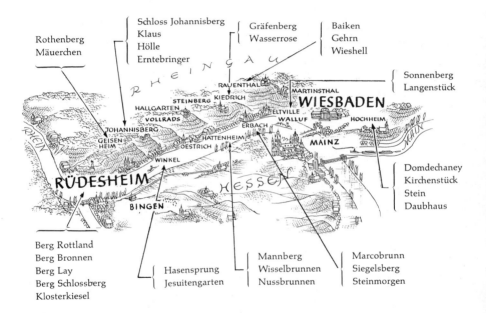

Rothenberg
Mäuerchen

Schloss Johannisberg
Klaus
Hölle
Erntebringer

Gräfenberg
Wasserrose

Baiken
Gehrn
Wieshell

Sonnenberg
Langenstück

Domdechaney
Kirchenstück
Stein
Daubhaus

Berg Rottland
Berg Bronnen
Berg Lay
Berg Schlossberg
Klosterkiesel

Hasensprung
Jesuitengarten

Mannberg
Wisselbrunnen
Nussbrunnen

Marcobrunn
Siegelsberg
Steinmorgen

THE RHEINGAU

illustrious, for there are fifty or sixty major producers in all, and of course literally hundreds of smaller ones.

A good many of these smaller growers, fortunately for us as well as for themselves, have set up cooperative cellars—*Winzervereine* and *Winzergenossenschaften*—and are thus able to afford the presses and other expensive equipment without which modern winemaking is scarcely possible. A list of such cooperatives and a reasonably complete roster of major growers has been included farther on in this chapter.

At the head of any such list, of course, must come the German State, which here, as in Hessia and on the Moselle, is by far the largest single vineyard owner, with some three hundred acres in the best towns and best *Lagen* of the whole Rheingau. The most interesting and most celebrated building of the Rheingau, Kloster Eberbach (an ancient, secularized Cistercian Monastery), is also state property, as are a whole series of modern cellars in Eltville, Rüdesheim, Hochheim, etc., all superbly equipped and magnificently run.

Compared to the other wine-growing districts of Germany, let alone those of France, the Rheingau is a very small area indeed, with less than 5000 acres of producing vineyard; the Moselle has four times, Hessia six times and the Pfalz seven times as much. But nowhere else is the average level of quality so high. To begin with, 72% of the vines are Rieslings and in all of the better *Lagen* there is practically nothing else; the 15% of Sylvaners and 8% of Müller-Thurgau being planted especially in Lorch, and in sections of heavy soil and lowland, for example around Hochheim and Oestrich. Second, the Rheingau's boundaries are so rigidly fixed by nature (Rhine on the south and cold, wooded hilltop on the north) that there is no possibility of the growers' expanding their plantings, even if they were tempted to do so. Third, and no one knows why, this seems to be one of those rare corners of the earth that ranks as a sort of vintner's Mother Lode, where sun and soil and one special variety of grape combine with man's help to produce a miracle which cannot be performed or repeated elsewhere.

In what might be called the geographical Rheingau—the lower slopes of the Taunus between where the Rhine turns west at Mainz, and where it turns north once more at Bingen; or, stated otherwise, between where it is joined by the Main and where it is joined by the Nahe—there are fourteen villages, nine strung along the river and five set back in the hills. The names of at least ten of the fourteen are well-known to wine-lovers the world over. Oddly enough, perhaps the most famous of all (and one which has given a portion of its name—"Hock," from the name "Hochheim"—to Rhine wines as a whole), is only in the Rheingau by courtesy, so to speak. It lies well to the east of the fourteen, and overlooks the Main, rather than the Rhine, but its wines are Rheingau wines all the same, not only legally, but in taste and flavor and class. Similarly, the villages of Lorch and Assmannshausen, both in the Rhine gorge north of Rüdesheim and Bingen, are rated as part of the Rheingau, and so is the big, popular resort of Wiesbaden, which has been an important American head-quarters ever since the war.

It must not be thought that even in so small a district as the Rheingau all the wines are alike or have more than a certain super-ficial family resemblance. Experts can name almost unfailingly the village that a particular wine comes from, and sometimes even the precise vineyard, or *Lage.* Each has its somewhat different character, and to tasters who live with them and see them daily they are as familiar as the faces of old friends. Thus the Hochheimers are mild and soft, sometimes with a trace of earthy taste, or *Bodenton;* the Rauenthalers are distinguished by their fruit, and an almost spicy quality of flavor; the good, familiar Eltvillers are well-balanced, con-sistently pleasing, rarely great; the Erbachers are sturdier, with more backbone, and the finest of them, the Marcobrunners, can be in-comparable; the wines of Hattenheim, which is just next door, run to finesse and delicacy and bouquet, whereas those of the Steinberg, on the hill behind Hattenheim, are forthright, masculine, overpower-ing, and in great years perhaps Germany's best. The Hallgarteners are extremely full-bodied, and I have heard them called "clumsy" and "graceless," although these are not wine-tasters' terms; the Johannis-bergers, and the best wines of Winkel, such as Schloss Vollrads, have great "elegance" and "distinction"—these are true wine-tasters' words, and high praise. The Geisenheimers have a rather special taste, by no means disagreeable but usually not too hard to recognize, and the Rüdesheimers, finally, are a law unto themselves; generally full and rich and fine, they rank in poor or fair years as the best of the Rheingau, but they are sometimes almost too heavy and too high in alcohol, with an underlying dryness, in years rated as great.

So much for a quick glance. The full story is a good deal more complicated as we shall soon see.

Here in the Rheingau, as on the Moselle, there are only a few of the great vineyards, or *Lagen* (three, to be exact: Schloss Vollrads, Schloss Johannisberg, and Steinberg), which are not partitioned, and which belong therefore to a single owner. This is much closer to the system which prevails in Burgundy than to that which prevails in Bordeaux, where Château Lafite is Château Lafite, and no nonsense about it. Here, therefore, the producer's name is quite as important as the vineyard name, and I am giving lengthy and rather detailed lists of the major producers for this exact reason. No such lists can hope to be complete, but there are certainly no major omissions in those farther on in this chapter.

And now to a closer examination of the Rheingau's towns:

*** *Hochheim,* a good ten miles east of the Rheingau proper, overlooks the Main, some three miles upstream from its junction with the Rhine. The country round about is gently rolling farm and orchard land, and Hochheim's 465 acres of vineyard form what amounts to an astonishing little island of vines in a district where there are no grapes at all. It is even more amazing that these vines, planted on relatively flat ground, as they are, yield wines which are not only comparable in quality to the Johannisbergers, for example, but which have the same essential characteristics of bouquet and texture and taste. For they are Rheingau wines and no mistake about it, and those from the eight or ten best vineyards—especially, oddly enough, in fair and good rather than great years—have the finesse and fruit and balance which are the marks of greatness in a wine. In Hochheim, more than in most other Rheingau towns, there is a striking difference between the wines of the better and those of the lesser vineyards. The former have an attractive softness; the latter, particularly in warm, dry years, lack class and have a disagreeable trace of commonness, sometimes even a soil taste, or *Bodenton.* The best *Lagen* (as their names would indicate) are those that directly adjoin Hochheim's pretty Gothic church, for Kirchenstück means "church-piece" and Domdechaney means "deanery."

No less famous than these, but certainly much less good, is the "Königen Viktoria Berg," which was named after Queen Victoria when she visited Hochheim in 1850. If, as has been reported, this was her favorite wine, as Bernkasteler Doktor was Edward VII's, the Queen had certainly a less good palate for German wines than her son, for the Viktoria Berg is a long way from being Hochheim's best vineyard.

The leading producers of Hochheim are as follows:

Domdechant (which means Dean) *Werner'sches Weingut.* 32 acres including holdings in almost all of the better *Lagen.*

Geh. -Rat Aschrott'sche Gutsverwaltung. 33 acres equally well placed.

Graf von Schönborn (see Hattenheim). Portions of Kirchenstück, Domdechaney, Rauchloch, Stein, etc.

Staatsweingut (the German State Domain—see Eltville). Holdings in Kirchenstück, Domdechaney and Stein.

Weingut der Stadt Frankfurt (the city of Frankfurt). 37 acres in the better *Lagen.*

Smaller producers of excellent reputation include a *Winzergenossenschaft* and a *Winzerverein,* also *Wilhelm Fischle Erben, Fürst Isenburg, Baron von Jungenfeld, Johann Quint* and *Paul Werle.*
And here, in approximately this order of quality, are the better vineyards:

Hochheimer Domdechaney	Hochheimer Kirchenstück
Hochheimer Rauchloch	Hochheimer Stein
Hochheimer Hölle	Hochheimer Daubhaus
Hochheimer Raaber	Hochheimer Stielweg
Hochheimer Sommerheil	Hochheimer Neuberg
Hochheimer Wiener	Hochheimer Gehitz
Hochheimer Steinern Kreuz	Hochheimer Beine
Hochheimer Königen-Viktoria-Berg	Hochheimer Hofmeister

Wiesbaden is such an attractive town, and remembered with affection by so many Americans, that it hardly seems fair to to say what I feel I must about its little vineyards, which consist of the Neroberg, plus one or two plots in Wiesbaden-Frauenstein. Both are technically part of the Rheingau, and the Neroberg is owned by the town of Wiesbaden itself. In Wiesbaden-Frauenstein, the *Groroler Hof* produces in great years some very creditable bottles. These, like the Nerobergers, are hardly worth exporting, but there is not much chance that we could get them even if we wished, for the thirsty burghers of Wiesbaden itself, aided, it must be admitted, by American officers, and by a good many thousands of tourists every year, drink them up in short order. There are only about 20 acres in the Neroberg, and some 80 in Wiesbaden-Frauenstein, so this is not as large an assignment as it sounds.

Martinsthal, until quite recently, was called Neudorf, and the old name still appears in many wine books and on many vineyard maps. The growers finally decided that the name Neudorf (which means "new village") had very little glamor on a wine label, and Martinsthal, it must be admitted, is an improvement. The village and its vineyards (173 acres) lie a mile or so back in the hills, not far from Rauenthal, and if the wines are a long way from equaling the astonishing quality of the Rauenthalers, they are creditable and sound, and in good years like 1953 have a considerable amount of bouquet and fruit. The principal producers are *J. B. Becker* (see the acknowledgment at the very beginning of this volume), the *Pfarrgut* and *Diefenhardt,* and the better *Lagen* are:

Martinsthaler Langenberg	Martinsthaler Pfaffenberg
Martinsthaler Heiligenstock	Martinsthaler Geisberg
Martinsthaler Steinberg	Martinsthaler Wildsau

* *Walluf.* This is another town name that has undergone a sea-change in the last decade. Formerly there was Oberwalluf and also Niederwalluf. The two still exist as villages, Niederwalluf with a little yacht harbor and a most agreeable restaurant terrace on the Rhine, Oberwalluf back up in its narrow valley on the way to Martinsthal. As far as their wines are concerned, both now are Walluf. The better *Lagen,* although little known, produce something quite excellent in good years, wines that are distinguished and fine; those from lesser vineyards often have a certain amount of "soil" taste, or *Bodenton.* The good producers are *J. B. Becker, Singer, Arnet Erben* and *Adam Scherer,* and the superior vineyards (87 acres in all) are:

Wallufer Walkenberg	Wallufer Unterberg
Wallufer Mittelberg	Wallufer Bildstock
Wallufer Steinritz	Wallufer Röderweg

** *Eltville's* 465 acres of vines make it one of the larger vineyard towns of the Rheingau, and most of these vines are part of a single unbroken *Weinberg,* extremely impressive in extent although not very steep, overlooking the Rhine just east of the town. A great deal of Eltviller is produced, and as a matter of fact, in the middle and lower price brackets, there is no better name to look for on German wine labels. The name is not famous enough to have been commercialized as yet, and the wines, if rarely sensational, are wonderfully consistent and pleasing, generally rather dry and fine and soft, with good bouquet—on the whole much better than the Hochheimers, Rüdesheimers and Johannisbergers that sell for the same money.

The town is substantial and busy, picturesque and very old. Its name does not, however, as some authorities have stated, come from the Latin *alta villa:* there were no towns on the right bank of the Rhine in Roman days, and Eltville was formerly called Ellfeld. Today it is to the wine trade what Rüdesheim is to the tourists—the Rheingau's unofficial capital—for in addition to several of Germany's most important *Sektkellerei,* or sparkling-wine houses, obvious and impressive on its main street, Eltville can also take pride in what is probably the most modern wine cellar in the world, that of the *Staatsweingut,* or State Domain, in two others hardly less famous but considerably more picturesque (Graf Eltz and Langwerth von Simmern) and in at least twenty smaller ones of honorable tradition and good name. Here is a brief list with a few details:

The *Verwaltung der Staatsweingüter im Rheingau,* or Administrative Office of the State Domains, is in Eltville, as are also the main storage and bottling cellars. These are, however, five separate State Domains, or *Staatsweingüter,* in the Rheingau, as follows: *Staatsweingut Rüdesheim, Staatsweingut Hattenheim-Erbach, Staatsweingut Rauenthal-Eltville-Kiedrich, Staatsweingut Hochheim, Staatsweingut Steinberg;* each of course has its own press-house and cellars. The vineyard holdings total 296 acres, including the Steinberg in its entirety, and parts, at least, of the best *Lagen* in all of the above named towns. The wines are mostly sold at auction, and except for those considered unworthy, are invariably estate-bottled, and shipped under the Domain's label and with the Domain's branded cork. Inferior wines, such as those of bad years and those that have to be "sugared," are sold off in bulk, generally without a vineyard name, to manufacturers of *Sekt.* The Domain's simple black and white label (black and white plus gold and red for Kabinett wines) is familiar to all wine-lovers; Kabinett wines are those that have been sold, either at auction or privately, at a predetermined, minimum, higher price per barrel or bottle.

Graf Eltz (Gräflich Eltz'sche Gustverwaltung). 68 acres of vineyard in Eltville, Rauenthal and Kiedrich. The Eltz family is one of the oldest of Germany and owned, before the war, enormous properties in Jugo-Slavia and Hungary, as well as their lovely and famous castle, Burg Eltz, on the Moselle, and the almost equally lovely Eltzerhof, or Schloss Eltz, here in Eltville. Jakob Eltz, the present Count, is young and active, speaks excellent English and has toured America. His wines are consistently of high quality. The name Schloss Eltz now appears on his labels, together with the town and vineyard designations.

Langwerth von Simmern (Freiherrlich Langwerth von Simmern'-sches Rentamt). 58 acres in Eltville, Hattenheim, Rauenthal and in the Marcobrunn of Erbach. The von Simmern home, and the cellars, are built around a beautiful, ancient, shady courtyard in the very center of Eltville. The wines, especially the Hattenheimers and the Marcobrunner, are of the very highest class, and the Simmern label, to my personal taste, is the most attractive of the Rhine.

Other producers of Eltviller wine, less important but of impeccable reputation, include *Jakob Fischer Erben* (20 acres), the *Lehr-und Versuchsweingut der Landwirtschaftskammer Hesse-Nassau,* a Provincial Wine School (18 acres), the *Stadtpfarrgut, R. C. Belz, Franz Boltendahl* and *Dr. Weil.* And the following small growers are worth noting: *Vowinkel Erben, Jakob Burg, J. B. Becker, Koegler, Ems, Jonas* and *Geschwister Offenstein.*

The best vineyards, in about this order:

Eltviller Sonnenberg	Eltviller Langenstück
Eltviller Klumbchen	Eltviller Mönchhanach
Eltviller Kalbspflicht	Eltviller Taubenberg
Eltviller Grauer Stein	Eltviller Sandgrub
Eltviller Weidenborn	Eltviller Freienborn
Eltviller Steinmacher	Eltviller Schlossberg
Eltviller Hahn	Eltviller Posten
Eltviller Albus	Eltviller Altebach
Eltviller Grimmen	Eltviller Setzling

*** *Rauenthal,* a modest and not particularly prepossessing little village, is some two miles north of Eltville, back in the Taunus Hills. The river road and the river traffic pass it by, and its wines, oddly enough, never seem to have found much favor with wine-drinkers outside Germany. This is indeed strange for at the famous wine auctions that take place every spring and fall in the Rheingau the Rauenthalers consistently bring higher prices than the wines of any other town, and in the opinion of a majority of German experts, they are not far from the Rheingau's best. It would certainly be hard to imagine anything much better than the 1949 and 1953 Rauenthalers of the State Domain, for example, although it must be admitted that unlike the wines of Rüdesheim, the Rauenthalers are anything but outstanding in off years.

I have before me as I write these lines the notes of two German friends (great *Weinkenner,* both of them) with whom I tasted a group of 1953 Rauenthalers a few years ago. Their comments were like a round of applause, and by the time we finished tasting there was a broad smile on the usually impassive face of Herr Direktor Jost, who is in charge of the Rheingau State Domains, and whose wines these were. For higher praise is hardly possible: *"pikante reife, feine Art, elegante Würze und Frucht, volle Frucht, edel feine Fülle, hochedle Frucht und Würze."* These terms are almost impossible to translate accurately, but one can say at least that distinction, ripeness and especially a piquant, an almost spicy sort of fruit and flavor, are more strikingly present in the Rauenthalers than in any other wines of the Rhine.

In addition to the State Domain (*Staatsweingut*), with holdings in Gehrn, Baiken, Wieshell, Wülfen, Pfaffenberg as well as other *Lagen,* major producers include *Freiherr Langwerth von Simmern* and *Graf Eltz* (for both, see Eltville). There is a *Winzerverein,* and the few good small growers include: the *Pfarrgut, Christian Sturm, Klein, Albus, Benedikt Russler* and *Wagner.*

Here are the more celebrated vineyards out of Rauenthal's 283 acres of vines:

Rauenthaler Baiken[1]	Rauenthaler Gehrn
Rauenthaler Wülfen	Rauenthaler Rothenberg
Rauenthaler Herberg	Rauenthaler Wieshell
Rauenthaler Burggraben	Rauenthaler Maasborn
Rauenthaler Hilpitzberg	Rauenthaler Pfaffenberg

[1] Rauenthaler Baiken is now classed, for tax purposes, as the most valuable agricultural land in Germany, even above the two most famous plots of Forst, in the Palatinate. This is to say that, in the opinion of experts, it is Germany's best vineyard. The experts are not far wrong.

Rauenthaler Steinhaufen	Rauenthaler Siebenmorgen
Rauenthaler Langenstück	Rauenthaler Nonnenberg
Rauenthaler Kesselring	Rauenthaler Huhnerberg

** *Kiedrich,* like Rauenthal, lies back in the hills behind Eltville and faces, across a narrow valley, an enormously impressive sweep of vines, crowned by the ruined castle of the Electors of Mainz, the Scharfenstein. It is an attractive town, with a pretty church and a famous old organ, and its wines, like those of Rauenthal, deserve to be better known outside Germany than they are, for those from its best vineyards (Gräfenberg and Wasserrose especially) can be truly remarkable in good years, with considerably more character and class than the wines of Eltville. The major producers include *Graf Eltz, Dr. Weil* (33 acres, mostly in Kiedrich), *Freiherr von Ritter zu Groensteyn* (important here as well as in Rüdesheim) and the *Staatsweingut.*

Among the good small growers are the *Pfarrgut, Barbeler, Brückmann, Gundlich, Martin Schreiber* and *Geschwister Bibo.* And the best-known *Lagen* (there are 320 acres in all):

Kiedricher Gräfenberg	Kiedricher Wasserrose
Kiedricher Sandgrub	Kiedricher Turmberg
Kiedricher Heiligenstock	Kiedricher Weihersberg
Kiedricher Dippenerd	Kiedricher Berg

*** *Erbach.* (320 acres.) Half a mile west of Eltville, and directly below Kiedrich, on the river, Erbach deserves top rating and three stars if only because of one vineyard, the Marcobrunn. This, one of the Rheingau's three or four most celebrated *Lagen,* is an absurdly narrow little strip of land, bounded by the river road, and bisected lengthwise by railway tracks. It lies off west of Erbach, beyond Schloss Reinhartshausen, the rather modest castle of Prince Friedrich of Prussia, on the way to Hattenheim, and it takes its name from a little fountain carved out of red sandstone and called the Marcobrunnen, or "boundary fountain," since it marks the boundary between Erbach and Hattenheim, the next village.

Officially the fountain, and the vineyard therefore, and the wine as well, belong to Erbach, not Hattenheim. And long ago a village poet of Hattenheim complained of the fact in couplets that have become famous and which, translated, say:

To solve this thorny question
Of what is yours, what mine . . .
Let Erbach keep the water
Give Hattenheim the wine.

This apparently is not the only dispute in which the Marcobrunn has been involved, for the half dozen producers who own portions of it consistently disagree as to how the vineyard name should be spelled and the wine listed. Although the fountain itself is inscribed "Marco-brunnen / Gemarkung Erbach," the wine is labeled "Erbacher Markobrunn" by Schloss Reinhartshausen, by the State Domain, by Kohlhaas and by von Oetinger, and simply "Marcobrunner" by Freiherr Langwerth von Simmern and by Graf Schönborn. However spelled, it is wholly admirable, in certain years (particularly dry years) perhaps the Rheingau's best, wonderfully balanced, with fruit, great breed, and a bouquet that can only be described as magnificent.

See note 4-1

The other Erbach wines, while excellent, are hardly of this superlative class; they are firm and fine, usually with a good deal of body, often somewhat hard. But they are well-knit, long-lived, and if they cannot stand comparison with the illustrious Marcobrunner, neither, it must be admitted, can most of the other wines of the Rhine.

All of the major producers listed below have holdings in the Marcobrunn and most of them in other Erbach vineyards as well:

Schloss Reinhartshausen (Prince Heinrich Friedrich von Prüssen). The wines are sold as "Schloss Reinhartshäusener Erbacher Markobrunn (or Erbacher Siegelsberg, etc.)" which scarcely has the virtue of making them easier to order from a wine waiter. This is the only important German producer who uses labels of entirely different colors to indicate different grades of wines: the lesser qualities carry a label of brilliant crimson, the middle grades one of brilliant, almost electric, blue, and the Cabinet (so spelled) label is white, with a narrow red border. The Domain consists of 74 acres of vines in Hattenheim and Erbach.

Freiherr Langwerth von Simmern. (See Eltville.)

Graf von Schönborn-Wiesenthied. (See Hattenheim.)

Staatsweingut. (The State Domain. See Eltville.)

Max Ritter und Edler von Oetinger. 13 acres in Erbach.

C. A. und H. Kohlhaas. 13 acres in Erbach.

Small growers worth of note include *H. Tillmanns Erben, Crass* and *Josef Kohlhaas,* and the following are the more important *Lagen:*

Marcobrunner (Erbacher Markobrunn)	Erbacher Siegelsberg
Erbacher Steinmorgen	Erbacher Brühl
Erbacher Honigberg	Erbacher Hohenrain
Erbacher Seelgass	Erbacher Rheinhell
Erbacher Michelmark	Erbacher Kahlig
Erbacher Bachhell	Erbacher Steinchen
Erbacher Hinterkirch	Erbacher Gemark
Erbacher Herrenberg	Erbacher Langenwingert
Erbacher Pellet	Erbacher Wormloch

*** *Hattenheim.* Of all the little towns of the Rheingau, Hattenheim is perhaps the prettiest, for there are dozens of quaint old half-timber houses clustered along its narrow streets, and a wide green meadow extends from the village down to the Rhine. With one outstanding exception, its best vineyards adjoin those of Erbach—Wisselbrunnen, Nussbrunnen and Mannberg are practically prolongations of the Marcobrunn, and produce wines of the same surpassing quality, although perhaps a little more delicate and less firm. The exception, and a major exception, is the incomparable Steinberg, a mile back of Hattenheim on its hill. This, together with its wonderful adjoining monastery, Kloster Eberbach, is technically within Hattenheim's town limits, but it is important enough to deserve treatment apart, and even without it, Hattenheim has its full share of good things. In bouquet, in those subtle qualities which go to make up what experts describe as "texture," in finesse, the best Hattenheimers of great years are simply unbeatable, and I, for one, have never tasted wines more flawless than the 1949 Hattenheimer Nussbrunnen Auslese of Langwerth von Simmern, or the 1953 Hattenheimer Engelmannsberg Spätlese of the State Domain. If the lordly Steinbergers can be called the kings of the Rheingau, these, surely, are the Rheingau's queens—feminine rather than powerful, but indescribably charming.

Hattenheim's most important cellars are those of *Graf von Schönborn-Wiesentheid,* where all of the wines of this Domain (the Rheingau's second largest—81 acres in all) are aged and bottled—not only Hattenheimers, but wines from Rüdesheim, Johannisberg, Erbach, Hochheim, etc. Other major producers include *Freiherr Langwerth von Simmern, Schloss Reinhartshausen,* the *Pfarrgut,* the

"Georg Müller Stiftung" (a charitable foundation now administered by the town of Hattenheim) and the *Staatsweingut,* or State Domain. And among the good smaller ones are *Adam Albert, Gossi, Gerhard, Diefenhardt* and *Ettinghausen.*

If experts the world over were asked to name Germany's greatest vineyard, it is more than possible that a majority would choose the *** *Steinberg:* Here, back of Hattenheim, as at Vougeot, in Burgundy, in France, Cistercian monks created, some seven hundred years ago, a unique, walled, hillside vineyard. Clos Vougeot today is divided among some sixty owners, but the 62-acre Steinberg is still intact—a single parcel, owned by the German State, cultivated and managed with the most scrupulous care. Although part of Hattenheim, its labels never so state, and its wines are sold simply and proudly as Steinberger, or Steinberger Kabinett, or Steinberger Spätlese Kabinett, or Auslese Kabinett, or Trockenbeerenauslese, etc.

Between these various grades and classes, rigorously kept separate and never blended, there are, of course, enormous differences, even in the wines of a given year. All of them will, to be sure, have a certain family resemblance, and to a greater or lesser extent the unmistakable Steinberger characteristics—full body, authority, great class, power and depth of flavor sometimes at the expense of subtlety, forthrightness sometimes at the expense of charm—but the wines labeled simply Steinberger may go to the consumer at $2 a bottle while the Trockenbeerenauslesen may bring, and have brought, $40 a bottle at auction. Steinberger 1953 is not one wine, but a dozen or more quite different wines and the designations that follow the name Steinberger on its label are of an importance hard to exaggerate. Below the grade of Kabinett (the indication of a wine that has sold at auction for a much higher price per barrel) Steinbergers are not likely to be distinguished; in extremely dry years like 1947 they sometimes have a trace of bitterness and lack fruit; in poor years like 1951 and 1954 they can be hard and unattractive. But when Nature smiles and conditions are favorable, in 1949 and 1953 for example, they are among the true glories of the Rhine.

The same Cistercian monks who created the Steinberg and surrounded it with its mile-and-a-half-long wall, also constructed in a wooded valley nearby a magnificent Gothic monastery, long since secularized, but remarkably preserved—Kloster Eberbach. This was actually founded by Augustinians in 1116, but was taken over by Cistercians, under the direction of St. Bernard de Clairvaux, less than twenty years later, and within a century had become the principal center of German viticulture and the German wine trade, with a branch in Cologne and a fleet of wine ships on the Rhine. Many of the wines of the German State Domain (the Steinbergers, among others) are aged and bottled in the old monastery buildings, which are extraordinarily picturesque with their vaulted ceilings and ancient wine-presses, and some of the major German wine auctions still take place there.

Including the Steinberg, Hattenheim has 475 acres of vineyard, and here is a list of the better *Lagen:*

Steinberg	Hattenheimer Wisselbrunnen
Hattenheimer Nussbrunnen	Hattenheimer Mannberg
Hattenheimer Engelmannsberg	Hattenheimer Hassel
Hattenheimer Willborn	Hattenheimer Hinterhausen
Hattenheimer Weiher	Hattenheimer Boden
Hattenheimer Pflänzer	Hattenheimer Gasserweg
Hattenheimer Stabel	Hattenheimer Kilb
Hattenheimer Dillmetz	Hattenheimer Klosterberg
Hattenheimer Bergweg	Hattenheimer Pfaffenberg
Hattenheimer Bitz	Hattenheimer Schützenhäuschen
Hattenheimer Boxberg	Hattenheimer Aliment
Hattenheimer Geiersberg	Hattenheimer Rothenberg

* *Oestrich,* with 750 acres, has the largest extent of vineyards of the Rheingau, a wide, gently sloping semicircle of vines extending along the Rhine for well over a mile, and swinging back into the hills to the west of Hallgarten. The wines are full-bodied, and not unlike those of Hallgarten but with considerably less class, soft, and in certain vintages even a little coarse. Lenchen is by all odds the best *Lage,* and the top producers are *J. Wegeler Erben, Mülhens-Berna* and the *Pfarrgut.* Smaller ones include *Gebrüder Walter, Fischbach, Steinmetz, Freymuth, Kunz, Fetzer, Kühn Erben, Eser* and *Johann Tillmann Erben.* The more important vineyard names are:

Oestricher Lenchen	Oestricher Doosberg
Oestricher Deez	Oestricher Klostergarten
Oestricher Eiserberg	Oestricher Pfaffenberg
Oestricher Hölle	Oestricher Räucherberg
Oestricher Kerbesberg	Oestricher Klosterberg
Oestricher Magdalenengarten	Oestricher Rosengarten

Mittelheim.   (310 acres.) A dull little town, producing full-bodied
wines of secondary quality. *Von Stoch, Baumer, Mülhens-Berna, Reitz, Anderson, Hupfeld Henner* and *Schönleber* are
reliable producers, and the best *Lagen* are:

Mittelheimer Oberberg	Mittelheimer Edelmann
Mittelheimer Neuberg	Mittelheimer Honigberg
Mittelheimer Stein	Mittelheimer Gottesthal
Mittelheimer Goldberg	Mittelheimer St. Nikolaus

** *Hallgarten* is another one of the upland villages, as distinguished
from the river towns of the Rheingau; it is about a half
mile west of Kloster Eberbach and some of its best vineyards are only
a stone's throw from the Steinberg. With such a situation, Hallgarten
could hardly fail to produce, especially in great years, wines of extraordinary quality, and the Hallgarteners of 1921, 1945 and 1949,
were and still are famous. They are tremendous wines, fuller in body
even than the Rüdesheimers, although drier, and generally with less
alcohol. The Hallgarteners of poor or fair years are another matter,
and I cannot say that I find them attractive.

The most important producer is Prince Löwenstein, or, as it
reads on the label, the *Fürstlich Löwenstein-Wertheim-Rosenberg'-
sches Weingut,* but *Karl Franz Engelmann* is quite in the same class,
and three cooperative cellars with rather amusing names also have
major holdings and produce good wine. These were founded during
the Boer War—the larger and richer growers formed the *Vereinigte
Weingutsbesitzer,* and were promptly called *"Die Engländer"* ("The
Englishmen") by their poorer neighbors, who formed their own
association, a *Winzergenossenschaft* named *"Die Buren"* ("The
Boers"). A third, a *Winzerverein* named *"Die Deutschen"* ("The
Germans") was formed later, and it seems to me rather to the credit
of the Rhinelanders that all three names survived two World Wars
and exist today. A few additional small producers worth noting: the
Pfarrgut, Josef and *Konrad Bug, Stettler, Strieht* and *Kremer.*

Hallgarten has 370 acres under vines and the best *Lagen* are:

Hallgartener Schönhell	Hallgartener Mehrhölzchen
Hallgartener Deutelsberg	Hallgartener Hendelberg
Hallgartener Rosengarten	Hallgartener Würzgarten
Hallgartener Jungfer	Hallgartener Kirschenacker
Hallgartener Deez	

*** *Winkel,* in German, means "angle" (as well as "nook" or "quiet corner") and the "angle," looking very much like a carpenter's square, appears in the coat-of-arms of Winkel, and on the wine labels of several of its good producers. In summer, at least, the village is anything but a "quiet corner," for it is practically indistinguishable from Mittelheim—two rows of houses strung along the noisy, busy, and unfortunately very narrow *Rheinstrasse,* the river road.

Winkel's greatest glory is *** *Schloss Vollrads,* the venerable and famous estate of the Matuschka-Greiffenklau family, a half mile back in the hills and reached by a narrow road up a long allée of poplar trees. This, with its 81 acres of vineyard, is the Rheingau's largest single, privately-owned domain, and one of its loveliest houses. Apart from the picturesque keep, or central tower, which dates from 1335, it is more of a manor house than a Schloss, or castle, built in the baroque style out of a red sandstone which goes wonderfully well with the green of the huge trees in its central courtyard, and the dark slate of its high roofs.

The present Graf Matuschka (who was pictured in the color pages of *Life* magazine not long ago, playing chess with his charming countess in the great hall of the Schloss) is president of the German Wine Producers Association; he personally and closely supervises both vineyard and cellar operations, and an idea of his high standards can be gained from the fact that, except for a few barrels, the entire Vollrads production of the disappointing 1954 vintage was sold in bulk, without the Vollrads label or name.

In good and great years (for this is a vineyard which requires sunshine) the wines of Vollrads are unsurpassed—they have ripeness, great fruit, and an extraordinary distinction. They are classified and labeled in a rather special way, which merits a few lines of explanation.

Schloss Vollrads, to begin with, does not market or ship a wine with the designation "Spätlese," although Auslesen, Beerenauslesen and Trockenbeerenauslesen are produced when growing conditions permit. Instead, Graf Matuschka divides his wines of below Auslese rank into three major and a whole series of minor categories, distinguishable by their labels and capsule colors. The lowest of these— honorable wines of middle quality—are sold simply as "Schloss Vollrads" plus the words *Original Abfüllung*; those of a higher class are marked (on the same basic label) "Schlossabzug" which means that they carry the Castle's stamp of estate-bottling (for the capsule colors,

See
note
4-2

see Page 148); finally the best (next to the Auslesen which, at Vollrads, are always of extremely high quality and always rather sweet)
are marked "Kabinett" and carry a blue capsule often with a stripe.
the capsules of the Auslesen are rose, of the Beerenauslesen white,
and the rare Trockenbeerenauslesen also carry a white capsule. The
last, produced in infinitesimal quantities and hard to come by, are
amazing wines. I still remember a bottle of 1920 Vollrads, Bestes
Fass, which I tasted at a dinner of the Société des Arts Gastronomi-
ques in Boston, many years ago; the 1945 was of the same great class,
and the 1959 which I last tasted a few months ago may prove better
than either. All were above criticism and beyond praise.

The prosaic little town of Winkel has four or five other vineyards
of almost equal distinction and fame (350 acres in all including Vollrads). Most of these (Hasensprung is the best of them) lie between
Schloss Vollrads and Schloss Johannisberg, and one could hardly rub
shoulders with better neighbors. The principal producers of Winkel
are as follows:

Graf Matuschka-Greiffenklau'sche Kellerei und Gutsverwaltung
—Schloss Vollrads.

Landgräflich-Hessisches Weingut (formerly Kommerzienrat Krayer Erben). 33 acres in Winkel and Johannisberg.

Von Brentano'sche Gutsverwaltung. 19 acres in Winkel.

Geromont'sche Gutsverwaltung. 10 acres in Winkel and Johannisberg.

Weingut Jakob Hamm. 10 acres in Winkel and Johannisberg.

There are at least a dozen smaller growers worthy of confidence:
the *Winzerverein, Eduard Krayer, Hans* and *Gerhard Blümlein, Jo-
hannes Grün, Sterzel, Faust, Derstroff, Kremer, Hennrich, Hofmann-
Eger* and *Christoph Petri.*
Winkel's best *Lagen:*

Schloss Vollrads	Winkeler Hasensprung
Winkeler Jesuitengarten	Winkeler Kläuserweg
Winkeler Honigberg	Winkeler Dachsberg
Winkeler Bienengarten	Winkeler Ansbach
Winkeler Klaus	Winkeler Oberberg

*** *Johannisberg* is by all odds the greatest name of the Rheingau. Whether it is the best wine can perhaps be argued, and even pleasantly and profitably argued, after the fashion of the French judge, who, being asked whether he preferred Burgundy or Bordeaux, replied, "My friends, this is a case in which the evidence on both sides is so interesting that I shall probably spend most of my life examining it, and allow my decision to be made public only after my death."

But it is a fact that even the Riesling grape is known in a number of countries, including Switzerland and the United States, as the Johannisberg, or Johannisberger, and when one speaks of Rhine wine, the name Johannisberger comes almost automatically to mind. And principally, of course, and first of all, *** *Schloss Johannisberg* itself.

There is no other vineyard quite like it, none with the same immensely regal look, as if it has been planned, on a vast scale, by some enormously talented landscape gardener. Its great steep hill, isolated, symmetrical, crowned with its castle, set in a sort of green amphitheater of the Taunus, is as dramatic as a stage setting, and whether seen from the river road, or from across the Rhine, dominates the whole landscape. The view from the castle terrace, whether by day or in the evening, is no less splendid—the vines fall away from the terrace edge like a green wave, and one has the impression that the Rhine, and its fertile, busy valley, are directly at one's feet.

It may or may not be true that it was Charlemagne himself who ordered the first vines planted on Johannisberg's steep hill. In any case, a Benedictine monastery had been constructed there by the year 1100, and when the church properties were secularized in 1801, it became the property of Prince William of Orange. The Congress of Vienna, after the fall of Napoleon, ceded it to the Emperor of Austria, and he in turn bestowed it as a fief on Prince Metternich, reserving, however, in perpetuity, one-tenth of its production of wine. This *Zehntel* (or *"Zehent"*) is still paid (though generally no longer in the form of wine) to the Habsburg heirs, by Fürst Paul von Metternich, the present owner.

The present castle is new, and as a matter of fact not completely finished. The previous Schloss was bombed with incendiaries by the R.A.F. during the War, and, except for its cellars, almost entirely destroyed. There are two versions of this bombing—one that the castle tower was being used as an anti-aircraft observation post and was attacked for that reason; the other that the bombers were attempting to hit a machine-tool factory, half a mile away on the

See note 4-3

"German vineyards, as a whole, are river vineyards and hillside vineyards." Along the Moselle between Enkirch and Zell.

"Where a plow can go, there no vine should grow."
Hand cultivation on the incredible hillsides of the Mittel-Rhein.

"A time of general rejoicing . . . " Harvesting Riesling grapes on the Rhine.

*An old Roman milestone on the
way from Piesport to Bernkastel.*

"Curving round like the inside of a great green bowl."
The village of Piesport and its incomparable vineyard slope. One is looking west.

"*Each individual vine, on the Moselle, has its stake, taller than a man*" — *some three thousand to the acre. Here, on the right, is what many experts call the greatest Moselle vineyard — Wehlener Sonnenuhr, which takes its name from the sundial (Sonnenuhr) visible above.*

The picturesque little town of Bernkastel. In the immediate foreground, part of the Bernkasteler Doktor vineyard.

*The extraordinary terraced vineyards of the Rüdesheimer Berg,
seen from across the Rhine. In the foreground, the town of Bingen; to the
left, the Nahe. Note the Ehrenfels, just above the church steeple.*

*A companion photograph to the above. The junction of Nahe
and Rhine, seen from the Rüdesheimer Berg. In the foreground,
the Ehrenfels; to the left, Bingen and the Scharlachberg vineyards.*

Schloss Vollrads, the venerable and famous estate of the Matuschka-Greiffenklau family. Here one is looking west. The Rhine is to the left and Schloss Johannisberg is directly behind the trees on the crest of the hill.

"No other vineyard has the same immensely regal look."
Schloss Johannisberg, *seen from the south-west.*

*"Let Erbach keep the water —
give Hattenheim the wine."
The Marcobrunn fountain and,
directly behind it, the famous
Marcobrunn vineyard. The
telegraph pole, visible on the
right, marks the railway line.
The Rhine is at one's back.*

*"The vine is cultivated with loving care . . . and what the
Riesling gives in return is beyond praise." A shrine in the vineyards, near Erbach, in the Rheingau.*

*"A magnificent Gothic monastery, long since secularized,
but remarkably preserved." Ancient wine-presses at
Kloster Eberbach, the home of Steinberger.*

"The Rheingau's unofficial capital" . . . *the picturesque half-timber houses of Eltville, with Eltviller Sonnenberg in the background.*

"Niersteins's better vineyards are directly on the river."
The "Rhine front" between Nackenheim and Nierstein. One is looking north-east.

"In Hessia . . . the vines are strung on wires and tailored until they look like
hedges in a formal garden." Oppenheim and its pretty Gothic church;
in the foreground, the famous Sackträger vineyard. One is looking north.

"In all probability this gave its name to Liebfraumilch . . ."
The Liebfrauenkirche, the Church of Our Lady, in Worms.

The steep vineyards of the Nahe Valley. Here is the Königsfels, at Schloss Boeckelheim.

"There are few happier people . . . than those who grow their grapes and make their wine." Here is some of the most valuable agricultural land in the world, the Kirchenstück and Jesuitengarten vineyards of Forst.

"Those picturesque and shining casks . . . the glory of German cellars."

The Würzburger Stein . . . "an extraordinary rocky hill within
the municipal limits of Würzburg."

"The Franconian vineyards are
almost all strung along the Valley
of the Main." Here are those
of Iphofen, among the best.

"The Neckar, between Stuttgart
and Heilbronn, is flanked
with vines." Terraced vineyards in Württemberg.

MOSEL-SAAR-RUWER

1953er

Scharzhofberger Spätlese

Gewächs von Egon Müller zu Scharzhof

Fuder Nr.

Original-Kellerabfüllung zu Scharzhof

MOSEL-SAAR-RUWER

1953er

Wiltinger Rosenberg

Auslese

Fuder Nr. 5307

Wachstum von Apollinar Joseph Koch

Original-Kellerabzug

1952er

Dom Avelsbacher

Herrenberg

Fuder Nr. 1

Originalabfüllung der Hohen Domkirche Trier

MOSEL-SAAR-RUWER

Weinbaugebiet

Mosel-Saar-Ruwer

1953er

Lieserer Niederberg Helden

feine Auslese Faß Nr. 360

Wachstum Freiherr von Schorlemer, Lieser an der Mosel

Mit Korkbrand abgefüllt in der Zentral-Kellerei Trier

VERBAND DEUTSCHER
NATURWEIN-
VERSTEIGERER E. V.

Unsere Mitglieder besitzen
Lagen von Weltruf.

V
D N
V

Dieses Zeichen
in Verbindung mit dem
Korkbrand verbürgt
naturreinen Wein.

TRIERER VEREIN VON
WEINGUTSBESITZERN
DER MOSEL, SAAR
UND RUWER

Wachstum

MOSEL-SAAR-RUWER

1953er

Wehlener Klosterlay

Auslese

Fuder Nr. 75
Original-Kellerabfüllung

S. A. Prüm Erben, S. A. Prüm, Wehlen, Mosel

VERBAND DEUTSCHER
NATURWEIN-
VERSTEIGERER E. V.

Unsere Mitglieder besitzen
Lagen von Weltruf.

V
D N
V

Dieses Zeichen
in Verbindung mit dem
Korkbrand verbürgt
naturreinen Wein.

TRIERER VEREIN VON
WEINGUTSBESITZERN
DER MOSEL, SAAR
UND RUWER

MOSEL-SAAR-RUWER
WINE

Bernkasteler Lay

Alcohol 9%
by Volume

1950er

Contents
1 Pint 8 Fl.Oz.

WACHSTUM Wwe. Dr. H. THANISCH
ORIGINAL-KELLER-ABZUG

1953er Rosalack
Schloss Johannisberger
Original Abfüllung der
Fürst von Metternich schen
Domäne.
Rheingau

Wappen der Fürsten
von Metternich - Winneburg

VERBAND
DEUTSCHER
NATURWEIN-
VERSTEIGERER E. V.

Unsere Mitglieder besitzen
Lagen von Weltruf!

RHEINGAU

1952er KABINETT
SCHLOSS VOLLRADS
WINKEL IM RHEINGAU
Graf Matuschka-Greiffenclau'sche Originalabfüllung

Rheingau
Schloss Reinhartshausener
CABINET
1949er Erbacher Markobrunn Auslese

Original- **RHEINGAU** Abfüllung

RHEINGAU
Kabinettwein
1949er
Steinberger
Auslese
NATURREIN
Verwaltung der Staatsweingüter
Eltville
Eigener Kellerabzug und Korkbrand

1952er Hochheimer
Daubhaus
Original-
Abfüllung
RHEINGAU
GEH. COMMERZIENRAT ASCHROTT'sche NACHLASSVERWALTUNG
GUT HOCHHEIM-VM.

RHEIN · HESSEN
1952er
Niersteiner Heiligenbaum
Spätlese
FASS No 217   NATURWEIN
REINHOLD SENFTER
WEINGUT NIERSTEIN OPPENHEIM u. DIENHEIM.
ORIGINAL-KELLER-ABFÜLLUNG

Faß 368
RHEINHESSEN
1953er NIERSTEINER KRANZBERG
Riesling Spätlese

Weingut Franz Karl Schmitt, Nierstein a. Rhein

Verwaltung der Staatlichen Weinbaudomänen Mainz
RHEINHESSEN
Edelgewächs
1953er
Niersteiner Auflangen
Riesling Beerenauslese
NATURREIN
Eigener Kellerabzug und
Korkbrand
Faß Nr. 33a

JULIUSSPITAL WEINGUT WÜRZBURG
1953er
Würzburger Leisten
Silvaner
FRANKEN
ORIGINALABFÜLLUNG

Originalabfüllung   Dr. Bürklin Wolf
Wachenheim an der Weinstraße
RHEINPFALZ
1953er
Wachenheimer Luginsland
Riesling Spätlese

Aus dem Weingute Geh. Rat Dr. v. Basser... mann-Jordan
Rheinpfalz Deidesheim
SIN VITE VITA
1953er Forster Jesuitengarten
Riesling Auslese
LAGE IM ALLEINIGEN BESITZ GEM. AMTL. KATASTER

ORIGINALABFÜLLUNG

Geisenheim road, and mistook their target. The reconstruction has been carried out with great good taste and the castle is quite as handsome as it was before.

The Schloss Johannisburg vineyard consists of 66 acres, directly in front of the castle, and its exposure could not conceivably be better. the press-house is modern, and the deep, vaulted cellars directly under the castle are models of what cellars should be.

Prince Paul Metternich is often absent and the day-to-day management of the estate is entrusted to the capable hands of Christian Labonte, whose signature appears on the labels, and who has been responsible for the introduction of certain modern techniques of agriculture and of wine making which have perhaps shocked a few traditionalists, but have proved eminently successful none the less.

It is nevertheless true that for nearly a decade—beginning with the 1954 vintage, which was poor everywhere, and ending with the 1962, which should have been better here than it was—Schloss Johannisberg went through a period of lean years. Its wines seemed somehow to have lost the special elegance which distinguished them; they were sound, even fine, Rheingau wines like their neighbors, but the old unmistakable superiority was no longer there. Happily, it is now possible to report that the eclipse is over and the bad days are past. In 1963 and again in 1964 there were no better wines made in the whole Rheingau than here, and the devoted partisans of Schloss Johannisberg have at last had their patience rewarded and their faith restored.

Perhaps the most flattering thing one can say about Schloss Johannisbergers when they are as they should be, is that they are worthy of their reputation, which is second to none. Less full-bodied than the Steinbergers, less overwhelming in fruit and flavor than the Marcobrunners, less piquant and spicy than the Rauenthalers, they are clearly the "first gentlemen" of the Rheingau, and their distinction, their class, is both obvious and incomparable.

Schloss Johannisbergers are sold under two quite different labels, and in addition to the usual designations of Spätless, Auslese, etc., of different categories and grades. Furthermore the term "Cabinet" is used here quite differently than by all other estates in the Rheingau.

First, and most important, is the standard Schloss label, with Labonte's signature and the Metternich *Wappen,* or crest. It is the capsule however, that indicates the quality, or grade. Lowest in the series is the red capsule, or Red Seal; next comes the Green (which may or may not be a Spätlese); higher still is the Rose, or Pink, generally a wine of at least Auslese rank.

The Cabinet label is quite different, and carries a drawing, in color, of the Schloss and its vineyard. It is used on wines marketed through different and special channels, wines not necessarily better but by no means less good than those that carry the Metternich coat-of-arms. Here again it is the capsule, or seal, that tells the story, and there exists a whole complicated succession of such seals (though many fewer than before the War), as follows: Orange Seal (approximately the equivalent of Red Seal, under the other label), White Seal (equals Green, above), *Himmelblau* or Sky-blue Seal (like Rose Seal) and Gold Seal, which is reserved for Beerenauslesen and Trockenbeerenauslesen.

Directly behind the Schloss, and out of sight of the river road, is the tiny village of Johannisberg, with 200 acres of vineyard surrounding the central 66 acres of the castle's Schlossberg. These, too, particularly in good years, produce wines of wonderful finesse and bouquet, often quite comparable in quality to those of the Metternich domain. The leading producers, all of them deservedly famous, are:

Landgräflich-Hessisches Weingut

G. H. von Mumm'sche Gutsverwaltung.

Geromont'sche Gutsverwaltung.

Graf von Schönborn-Wiesentheit.

Less important, but well worth noting, are a number of good small growers such as *Jakob Hamm, Karl Zerbe, Peter Schamari Erben, Moos Erben, Eser, Jakob Hofmann, Kauter Erben, Kempenich* and *Josef Klein Erben.*

And the outstanding vineyards are, more or less, in this order:

Schloss Johannisberg (Johannisberger Schlossberg)

Johannisberger Klaus	Johannisberger Sterzelpfad
Johannisberger Kläuserpfad	Johannisberger Hölle
Johannisberger Kochsberg	Johannisberger Kerzenstück
Johannisberger Kahlenberg	Johannisberger Hansenberg
Johannisberger Vogelsang	Johannisberger Weiher
Johannisberger Mittelhölle	Johannisberger Nonnhölle
Johannisberger Unterhölle	Johannisberger Steinhölle
Johannisberger Goldatzel	Johannisberger Schwarzenstein

Johannisberger Erntebringer

** *Geisenheim* is even more celebrated for its school, the *Lehr-und Forschungsanstalt fur Wein-, Obst- und Gartenbau,* than for its wines, excellent as these latter are. This "School-and-Research-Institute-for-Viticulture-Fruit-culture-and-Horticulture," as it is succinctly called, is one of the great wine schools of the world, and responsible in no small measure for the extraordinarily high level of wine technology in Germany. The school property includes extensive vineyards from which the wines are made, as might be expected, with scrupulous care, and the school label is one of the most respected of the Rheingau. The town is prosperous and attractive, with a Gothic cathedral, a castle belonging to Graf Schönborn, and a famous 600-year-old linden tree.

The vineyards extend from within a few hundred yards of Schloss Johannisberg to what used to be the village of Eibingen, and is now part of Rüdesheim, or for nearly two miles; they comprise 485 acres.

Like the Rüdesheimers, the wines of Geisenheim have the considerable virtue of being good and sometimes even excellent in vintage years ranked as fair; unlike most Rüdesheimers, they achieve surprising heights in great years as well and the Beerenauslesen and Trockenbeerenauslesen of Geisenheim rank with the very best. A Geisenheimer Mäuerchen, for example, was rated as the Rheingau's finest wine in the superb 1893 vintage, and the 1945s, too, were remarkable.

Leading producers include *Lehr- und Forschungsanstalt, Josef Berger Erben,* the *Weingut Rebhof (Theo Soherr), Zobus Erben, Freiherr von Zwierlein Erben* and *Graf von Schönborn.* And among the smaller growers: *Kohmann, Hebauf, Rammersbach Erben, Dr. Werthmann Erben, Phillip Graf, Karl Gimbel* and *Jakob Holschier.* The best vineyards:

Geisenheimer Rothenberg	Geisenheimer Mäuerchen
Geisenheimer Katzenloch	Geisenheimer Lickerstein
Geisenheimer Klauserweg	Geisenheimer Fuchsberg
Geisenheimer Fegfeuer	Geisenheimer Marienberg
Geisenheimer Mönchspfad	Geisenheimer Morschberg
Geisenheimer Altbaum	Geisenheimer Rosengarten
Geisenheimer Decker	Geisenheimer Hinkelstein
Geisenheimer Kreuzweg	Geisenheimer Kosakenberg
Geisenheimer Kirchgrube	Geisenheimer Kilsberg

*** *Rüdesheim* is the westernmost town of the Rheingau proper— beyond it not even an Arizona cliff-dweller would attempt to construct a village. Its principal buildings and main streets occupy the last few acres of flat land at the foot of the Rüdesheimer Berg, and some of its narrow *Gassen,* or alleys, wind and clamber like the streets of a hill town in Italy.

Seen from across the river, from Bingen, at the mouth of the Nahe, Rüdesheim and its Berg present an extraordinary and impressive picture: a smiling and pretty little town; next to it and behind it, an almost perpendicular hill, cut and terraced into what looks like a gigantic stairway, with wall above wall above wall, each supporting its little patch of vines, as the vineyards climb on past Rüdesheim's ruined castle, the Ehrenfels, to the trees of the Niederwald at the hill's crest.

The Rhine, once it has been joined by the Nahe, picks up speed, and narrows, then swings in a great swift curve around the Rüdesheimer Berg to plunge into the veritable canyon through which it runs northward to Coblenz. This stretch of fast and often turbulent water, dangerous and difficult to navigate, is the so-called "Binger Loch," the "Hole of Bingen," and on a little island a picturesque old tower, the Mauseturm, stands guard over it. Near here, too, are the famous "Hunger Stones"—rocks in the bed of the Rhine that are visible only in years of extreme drought and low water—their appearance is supposed to presage a poor harvest, but great wine.

Situated in a sort of bottle-neck of road and rail and river traffic, Rüdesheim was heavily bombed and badly damaged in the War, although its great railway bridge over the Rhine survived, and was only destroyed by the retreating German army, at the end. Many of the good vineyards too were severely battered but they and the town itself have largely been restored, and Rüdesheim is once more a major tourist and excursion center, as in pre-War days. An auto-ferry runs across to Bingen, there are passenger steamers in both directions on the Rhine, and a new cable railway carries its baskets of visitors high over the vineyards to the Niederwald. Here a hotel and restaurant have been installed in what was once the hunting lodge of the Dukes of Nassau, and here, too, is the National Denkmal, the "Germania Monument," a graceless pile if there ever was one, which, however, commands a truly magnificent view over the Rhine Valley.

Most of Rüdesheim's best vineyards (there are 650 acres in all) are somewhat west of the village, on the terraced face of the Berg, and wines from these have the word "Berg" as part of their name, as Rüdesheimer Berg Rottland, for example, but *not* Rüdesheimer Klosterkiesel, nor Rüdesheimer Hinterhaus. These Berg wines have the typical Rüdesheimer characteristics to a pronounced degree: an extraordinary richness and ripeness, full body, a somewhat more golden color than most other Rheingau wines, slightly more alcohol, somewhat less finesse. Because of the incomparable exposure of the vineyards, and the shallow, rocky soil on which they are planted, the vines often suffer from drought, particularly in great or sunny years. In vintages considered fair or good, the Rüdesheimers are frequently the best wines of the Rhine; in great vintages they are often less outstanding, lacking in balance and sometimes in fruit, and this is even more true of the Berg wines than of the others. Many of the 1950 Rüdesheimers were better than the '49s, and in a year ranked as superlative, Klosterkiesel may produce finer wine than Berg Bronnen, although the latter is certainly the better *Lage*.

The vineyards of *Graf Franken-Sierstorpff*, formerly the most important of Rüdesheim, were broken up and sold a few years ago, and the top producers are not very numerous today, nor are their holdings very large. All of the following, however, produce wines of the highest class, and their labels can be counted on absolutely:

Freiherr von Ritter zu Groensteyn. This estate is now usually known as Schloss Groensteyn. Important holdings in Berg Mühlstein, Berg Bronnen, Berg Paares, Berg Hellpfad, Berg Rottland, Bischofsberg, Hinterhaus, etc.

Staatsweingut (the State Domain). Important acreage in Berg Schlossberg, Berg Rottland, Bischofsberg, Klosterkiesel, etc.

Graf von Schönborn. Large vineyards in Berg Zollhaus, Berg Bronnen, Berg Roseneck, Bischofsberg, etc.

Geh.-Rat Jul. Wegeler Erben. Important properties in Berg Burgweg, Berg Rottland, Berg Bronnen, Berg Roseneck, Berg Schlossberg, Hinterhaus, etc.

Fritz Rücker Erben. Small but excellent holdings in Berg Rottland, Berg Hellpfad, Berg Roseneck, Berg Bronnen, Bischofsberg, etc.

Julius Espenschied. Small but excellent holdings in Berg Burgweg, Berg Rottland, Berg Lay, Berg Hellpfad, Bischofsberg.

There are a good number of dependable smaller growers. For example: the *Pfarrgut,* the *Frühmessereigut, Anton Barth, Johann Petri, Robert Trapp, Philipp Veith, Philipp Bibo Erben, Wallenstein*

Erben, Dadischek, Geschwister Hepp Erben, Philipp Keutner, Josef Philipp, Johann Müller and *Jakob Lill IV.*

The following are the celebrated vineyards, and they rank more or less in this order:

Rüdesheimer Berg Rottland	Rüdesheimer Berg Bronnen
Rüdesheimer Berg Roseneck	Rüdesheimer Berg Hellpfad
Rüdesheimer Berg Lay	Rüdesheimer Berg Schlossberg
Rüdesheimer Berg Mühlstein	Rüdesheimer Berg Zollhaus
Rüdesheimer Bischofsberg	Rüdesheimer Klosterkiesel
Rüdesheimer Berg Burgweg	Rüdesheimer Berg Stumpfenort
Rüdesheimer Berg Paares	Rüdesheimer Hinterhaus
Rüdesheimer Berg Platz	Rüdesheimer Berg Dickerstein
Rüdesheimer Berg Kronest	Rüdesheimer Engerweg
Rüdesheimer Wilgert	Rüdesheimer Hasenlaufer
Rüdesheimer Berg Stoll	Rüdesheimer Berg Eiseninger
Rüdesheimer Berg Ramstein	Rüdesheimer Berg Katerloch
Rüdesheimer Linngrub	Rüdesheimer Häuserweg

Assmannshausen lies north of the Binger Loch, beyond the Rüdesheimer Berg, and for a boatman it is therefore outside the Rheingau, whatever we wine-drinkers may say. Actually, in terms of wine, too, it is a region apart, since it produces red wine to the virtual exclusion of all else. This, red Assmannshäuser, has been dealt with in another chapter, and perhaps we may usefully add here only a few facts concerning the vineyards and producers.

The vineyards (180 acres) are directly north of, and parallel to, those of Rüdesheimer Berg; they are on a slope almost equally steep, overlooking a little side valley running back to Aulhausen, behind the National Denkmal and the Niederwald. They are planted almost exclusively to the Pinot Noir (here called the Spätburgunder) cuttings of which were brought from France by St. Bernard de Clairvaux over eight hundred years ago. Outside of one excellent hotel, the Krone, there is nothing much to the town. By a very large margin, the most important producer is the State Domain, or *Staatsweingut;* smaller growers with a good reputation include *Hufnagel, Wittman, Jung, Eulberg, Bohnert* and *Brühl.* Note:

Assmannshauser Höllenberg   Assmannshauser Hinterkirch
Assmannshauser Frankenthal

Lorch and *Lorchhausen.* Here, north of Assmannshausen, the official Rheingau comes to what can only be described as a rather inglorious end. One excellent producer, *Graf von Kanitz,* makes excellent wine at Lorch, but the soil and growing conditions, even in the best *Lagen* (Pfaffenweis, Bodenthal, Krone), are quite different and, however good, these are Rheingau wines in name only and could better be described and listed as the outstanding products of another and adjoining district, the Mittel-Rhein. It may be worth adding, however, that Lorch and Lorchhausen together have over 720 acres of vines.

V

HESSIA

(Rheinhessen)

Hessia, or Rheinhessen, is a little rectangle of rather bare, rolling country, about thirty miles by twenty, bounded on the east and north by the Rhine and on the west by the Nahe. An old Roman road runs diagonally across it and the cities of Worms and Mainz and Bingen mark three of its four corners; all three are on the Rhine. From a wine-lover's standpoint, the fourth corner matters not at all, since all of the really great Hessian vineyards either overlook the Rhine or are close to the Rhine, and what there is of interest to the west and south-west belongs to the Nahe, which is another district and of which more later.

Hessia, as far as Americans are concerned, is perhaps best known for its Hessians, those mercenary soldiers of the King (fortunately for us, not too good ones) in our Revolutionary War, or War of Independence. But this is not the whole story by any means. Gutenberg, the father of printing, was born and died in Mainz. Worms is famous for its "Diet of Worms" which, as I learned long ago, to my considerable disappointment as a schoolboy, does not mean what it seems to and is connected instead with the history of the Reformation. Bingen, in turn, is celebrated for its "Bingen pencils," which is another and amusing word for "corkscrews" in colloquial German. A surprisingly large number of the Germans who came to

84

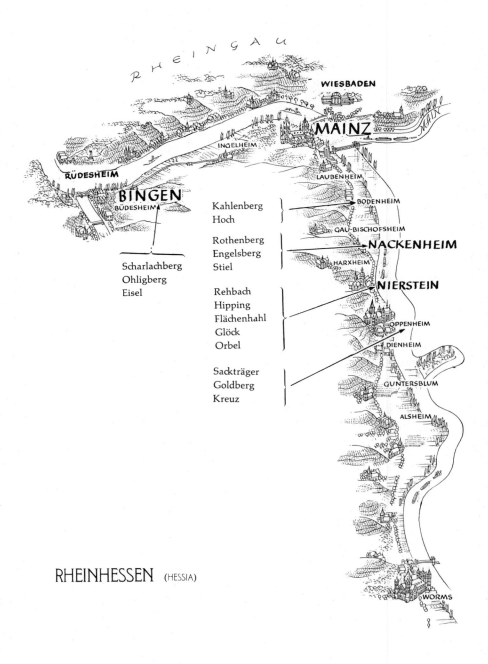

RHEINHESSEN (HESSIA)

America during the 19th Century were from Hessia, and finally, of course, Hessia is the home of Niersteiner and Liebfraumilch. It could almost properly be called Liebfraumilchsheim.

Just as a matter of record, there are 155 villages in Rheinhessen which produce wine; it is safe to say that 99% of them produce Liebfraumilch, or something eventually sold as such; what is more astonishing is that 120 out of the 155 have names that end in "heim." Home, or "heim," is something important to all of us, but this would seem excessive, and it is certainly confusing. The custom has spread to neighboring provinces, witness Rüdesheim in the Rheingau, Norheim on the Nahe, Deidesheim and Wachenheim in the Pfalz, and even, to go farther afield, Bergheim in Alsace and Anaheim in Southern California. But the Hessians are easily the champions.

"Home" and "Mother" are so often coupled together in common speech that it is hardly surprising to find Hessia (the home of "heim") specializing in a wine called "Milk of the Blessed Mother," for this, precisely, is what Liebfraumilch means.

And, precisely, it is all it means.

Originally it may have been or was, as many have claimed and some have tried to prove, a wine produced in the little vineyard round the Liebfrauenkirche, the Church of our Lady, in Worms. It is still that, but it is also every other white wine produced in Rheinhessen if its producer cares to so sell it, a splendid wine or a poor one, a wine as dry as Chablis or as sweet as Sauternes, a wine that costs $4 a bottle and is worth it, or one that is no bargain at 98¢. The name has simply no standing whatever under German law, and practically anything that can be sold as wine can be called Liebfraumilch. The consumer's guide and his only guide, other, of course, than vintage and such terms as Spätlese, Auslese, and the like, is the shipper's name. This may or may not be the producer's name *and in most instances is not.*

The Hessian wines, like those of the Rheingau and the Nahe, as well as those of the Pfalz, come in brown bottles, and apart from those called Liebfraumilch, they are labeled according to the same system—town plus vineyard name, *Original-Abfüllung* and all the rest—as other German wines.

Grown as they are on quite different soil from that of the other great vineyard districts of the Rhine, the wines of Hessia have a distinct character of their own, an attractive softness, at once light and mild. When this is combined with distinction and fruit and real finesse, as in the wines of Nierstein and Nackenheim, and the better of those from Bingen and Oppenheim and (more rarely) from Bodenheim and Dienheim, the result is very charming. Here you will find none of the austerity of the wines of the Saar, nor yet of the overwhelming power and flavor of the greatest Rheingaus. But there are times when Mendelssohn is more welcome than Bach or Wagner. And so it is with the wines of Rheinhessen.

Here, as elsewhere in Germany, the best wines are those that come from the Riesling grape, but the overwhelming majority of Hessian wines are made from the Sylvaner; actually, of the 30,000 acres of vineyard in the little province, about two-thirds are planted to Sylvaners, perhaps 10% to Müller-Thurgaus, some 15% to lesser varieties, mostly red, and not over 10% to Rieslings. Fortunately, the latter are concentrated in the best vineyard towns and best *Lagen.*

Of the 155 wine-producing villages of Hessia, there are only about a dozen that need concern us here, possibly even less. All of them are on the Rhine, or at least on the escarpments that overlook the Rhine Valley. With the single and notable exception of Bingen, with its Scharlachberg, or "scarlet hill," at the mouth of the Nahe, all of them lie along what they call the "Rheinfront," south of Mainz. Most of them share, to a greater or lesser extent, the typical red sandstone soil (very unlike the dark basalt of the Pfalz, the black slate of the Moselle, and the golden-brown soil of the Rheingau) and all of them produce wines that have a good deal in common. There is unfortunately a vast acreage in the interior, in and around the valley of an insignificant little river called the Selz, or elsewhere, generally on heavy clay soil which perhaps could better be planted to potatoes than to grapes. This is the source of most of the cheap and common Liebfraumilchs to which experts take exception—if shipped under the name of their town and vineyard, rather than under the familiar, all-embracing, common name of Liebfraumilch, they would be more easily recognized for what they are.

Here is a little summary of the leading wine towns of Hessia and their vineyards:

The city of *Mainz,* long one of the principal centers of the German wine trade, actually owns a vineyard or two of its own, just as Frankfurt does, and Wiesbaden, and incidentally both Lausanne and Neuchâtel, in Switzerland. I am ashamed to say that I have never tasted Mainzer Michelsberg—judging by what I have been told by friends whose opinion I trust, I have not missed anything of major value. Nevertheless *Die Stadt Mainz* is officially a member of the V.D.N.V., the great association of German estate-bottlers, and wines are sold at auction under its label. Most of these come from two secondary towns well back from the Rhine, and the Michelsberg, which is within the city limits, consists of only about four acres.

Mainz, however, is far more important as the headquarters and central office of the *Staatliche Weinbaudomäne* of Rheinhessen, an extraordinary group of vineyards owned by the German State. Here, as in the Rheingau, these include holdings in almost every major wine-producing town, with a total of 180 acres, and what they bottle is of the highest possible class. The *Domäne* has its press-houses and complete cellar establishments in Bodenheim, Nackenheim, Nierstein, Oppenheim (which takes care of the wines of Dienheim as well), and Bingen; the wines are sold at auction and generally packed and shipped in Mainz (after estate-bottling either at the vineyard or in Mainz). They all carry a rather unusual diamond-shaped label, much like that used on the State Domain wines from the Moselle and Saar.

Laubenheim, with some 300 acres under vines, is the first vineyard town of real consequence as you go southward along the "Rhine front" from Mainz to Worms. Its name is one that used occasionally to appear on wine lists in England and America before the First World War—it would be hard to say why, unless the wines of those days were a great deal better than what is now being produced. Small, soft, rather common, the Laubenheimers are a long way from top rank.

* *Bodenheim* marks the real beginning of the fine wine country. Its eminence is due, as far as modern times are concerned, principally to the efforts of two vineyard-owners, the heirs of the late Lieutenant-Colonel Liebrecht, and the State Domain. Both have important holdings on the hillsides well back from the alluvial soil along the river and both produce wines with little or none of the heavy, earthy flavor (called *Bodenton* or *Bodengeschmack*) which are often present in the lesser vintages of this rather unfortunately named village. The truth is of course that these deprecatory terms have only an accidental connection with the name of Bodenheim; they can more accurately be used in describing the wines of at least half a hundred other towns which go to market, like many Bodenheimers, as "Liebfraumilch."

The two leading producers, as mentioned above, are the *Oberst-leutnant Liebrecht'sche Weingutsverwaltung* and the *Staatsweingut Bodenheim;* both, in years such as 1949 and 1953, produce some extraordinary wines. There are 650 acres of vines, with a small proportion of Rieslings. The better *Lagen,* or individual, named vineyards are:

Bodenheimer Hoch	Bodenheimer Kahlenberg
Bodenheimer St. Alban	Bodenheimer Silberberg
Bodenheimer Braunloch	Bodenheimer Leidhecke
Bodenheimer Westrum	Bodenheimer Kapelle
Bodenheimer Bock	Bodenheimer Sandkaut
Bodenheimer Burgweg	Bodenheimer Ebersberg
Bodenheimer Mönchpfad	Bodenheimer Rettberg

*** *Nackenheim* is perhaps the equivalent, in Rheinhessen, of what Rauenthal is in the Rheingau: the perennial and beloved favorite of experts, a village which, for some odd reason, beyond the frontiers of Germany, has never been famous at all. The vineyards of course are not very large; the best of them form the northern cusp of that extraordinary crescent of red hillside soil overlooking the Rhine which has made the reputation and the glory of Nierstein. This is the finest wine-producing land of Hessia, and unfortunately there is precious little of it; it is unmistakable, and as red as brick. Nackenheim's portion is very small indeed, surely under a hundred acres, and it is not by chance that the best vineyard of all is called Rothenberg, or "red hillside." The three "great" estates listed below are actually holdings of between twelve and thirty acres and sell their annual output so easily that they scarcely need to try to develop an export market for their wines. These wines, apart from the very best Niersteiners, are certainly unsurpassed in the whole province, they have great bouquet, and are remarkable for what German experts call "elegance"—unusual finesse and class.

Nackenheim has only 240 acres under vines, about a third of them Rieslings, but here even the Sylvaners seem to surpass themselves. The leading producers are: *Gunderloch-Lange, Gunderloch-Usinger, Staatsweingut Nackenheim.*

There is also an important and well-run *Winzergenossenschaft,* and here are the better *Lagen:*

Nackenheimer Rothenberg	Nackenheimer Engelsberg
Nackenheimer Stiel	Nackenheimer Fenchelberg
Nackenheimer Rheinhahl	Nackenheimer Kapelle
Nackenheimer Fritzenhöll	Nackenheimer Spitzenberg

*** *Nierstein* is easily the foremost wine town of Hessia—first in fame, first by far in total production, and first in quality as well. It is a busy and cheerful little place, with a mineral spring, the *Sironabad,* which was known even in Roman days, and an important anchorage much used by Rhine barges. The town and the better vineyards are directly on the river and it is believed that the reflected morning sunlight off the Rhine plays a major role in the development of that extraordinary ripeness which is the distinguishing mark of the best Niersteiners. These are very great wines indeed, quite different in character from those of the Rheingau and the Pfalz, but in the same noble class.

There is an old saying that all Liebfraumilchs would be Niersteiners if they could, and it is fairly safe to assume that the really distinguished ones (and there are such) are either straight from some good Nierstein vineyard, or are blends of Niersteiner and something else. The careful and scrupulous local producers are always a little baffled to discover that what they have laboriously kept separate is often more acceptable, in certain outlandish distant countries, when mixed together, and that town and vineyard names which they consider patents of nobility, proofs of excellence and justifications of high price, are so little regarded abroad that a Niersteiner Rehbach is sometimes sold more readily as "Liebfraumilch" than under its own proper and proud name.

This is not at all to say that everything that Nierstein produces is great wine, for such is a long way from being the case. Well over half of the 1340 acres of vineyard are in Sylvaner, and all of the celebrated *Lagen* are on two narrow hillsides—most of them on the *Rheinfront,* facing southeast along the river, the others in the *Tal,* facing almost due south over a shallow tributary valley. In the case of no other German wine, therefore, is a vineyard name so important. Nierstein's average production is in the neighborhood of 400,000 gallons a year, of which, of course, a good share is consumed locally and never bottled at all, and a substantial part labeled simply Niersteiner or Liebfraumilch. The cream, marketed under a vineyard name, amounts to not over 15% or 20%.

Four producers and estate-bottlers are internationally known, and the label of any one of the four is almost in the nature of a diploma. These are *Franz Karl Schmitt, Freiherr Heyl zu Herrnsheim, Reinhold Senfter* and the *Staatsweingut.* In addition there is a well-run *Winzergenossenschaft,* and about a dozen reputable small growers also bottle their wine: *Dieterich, Fritz & Josef & Martin*

Schwibinger, Seebrich, Georg & Heinrich Seip, Steib, Strub, Vowinkel Erben and *Wehrheim.*
The better *Lagen,* in about this order:

Niersteiner Rehbach	Niersteiner Auflangen
Niersteiner Hipping	Niersteiner Flächenhahl
Niersteiner Glöck	Niersteiner Kehr
Niersteiner Orbel	Niersteiner Kranzberg
Niersteiner Floss	Niersteiner Streng
Niersteiner Pettental	Niersteiner Oelberg
Niersteiner Heiligenbaum	Niersteiner Brudersberg
Niersteiner Fuchsloch	Niersteiner Gutes Domtal
Niersteiner Schnappenberg	Niersteiner Rohr
Niersteiner Spiegelberg	Niersteiner Hölle
Niersteiner St. Kiliansberg	Niersteiner Fockenberg

** *Oppenheim,* an exceedingly picturesque and pretty little town, with a fine Gothic church, is set on a low hill well back from the river, and commands a charming view over the green fertile bottomland of the Rhine Valley. The 450 acres of vineyard, about a third Rieslings, are mostly south of the town, on gently sloping soil that falls away toward Dienheim and the flat plain in the direction of Worms.

Not long ago, in an old book on the wines of Hessia, I ran across a description of the wines of Oppenheim obviously written by one of their most faithful lovers and most determined champions. Practically every favorable adjective in the German language, conceivably applicable to wine, is included, and the list runs as follows: *"rassig, reintönig, reingärig, elegant, sauber, spritzig, stahlig, blumig, saftig, bukettreich, glatt, kernig, süffig, vollmundig, duftig, zart, rund, reif, gross, hochedel."* Obviously no such paragon among wines ever existed, let alone in Oppenheim, although the best Oppenheimers can be very good indeed, soft and ripe and full, but with less breed and less distinction than the wines of Nierstein.

The leading producers are the *Weingut der Stadt Oppenheim* (the town of Oppenheim, itself) the *Landes-Lehr- und Versuchanstalt* (a Provincial wine school) and the *Staatsweingut Oppenheim* (the State Domain). Other good and dependable small growers include *Bayer, Gallois, Jungkenn Erben, Carl Koch Erben, Wallot* and *Winter.*

And the better vineyards:

Oppenheimer Kreuz	Oppenheimer Sackträger
Oppenheimer Herrenberg	Oppenheimer Goldberg
Oppenheimer Steig	Oppenheimer Reisekahr
Oppenheimer Kröttenbrunnen	Oppenheimer Zuckerberg
Oppenheimer Daubhaus	Oppenheimer Schlossberg
Oppenheimer Herrenweiher	Oppenheimer Kehrweg

* *Dienheim,* something over a mile farther south on the road to
Worms, is Oppenheim's immediate neighbor, and within
its communal limits are portions of two of Oppenheim's best *Lagen,*
Kröttenbrunnen and Goldberg. The average quality of the wines,
however, is considerably lower, and of some 925 acres of vineyard,
a large part is on the plain. The three leading producers mentioned
above, in connection with Oppenheim, are also the best of Dienheim
—the *Weingut der Stadt Oppenheim,* the *Landes-Lehr- und Versuchanstalt* and the *Staatsweingut.*
     The better vineyards:

Dienheimer Goldberg	Dienheimer Guldenmorgen
Dienheimer Kröttenbrunnen	Dienheimer Tafelstein
Dienheimer Rosswiese	Dienheimer Siliusbrunnen

Guntersblum, in vineyard acreage, is second only to Nierstein in
all Hessia, but I have not often seen a wine labeled
Guntersblumer and most of what its 990 acres produce is marketed
locally, or as Liebfraumilch.

Alsheim, in quality, is perhaps a shade better, and I find in my
tasting notes some quite favorable comments on certain
Alsheimers of the 1953 vintage. There are 590 acres of vines.

* *Worms,* before the War, was a pleasant small city of red sandstone buildings and a green belt of grass and trees had
replaced most of its old walls; unfortunately it was also a focal point
of rail and road traffic along and across the Rhine. As such it was
heavily bombed, to the point that it was hardly recognizable in 1945.
It has been partly, but by no means entirely, rebuilt.
     To the casual visitor, Worms looks about as unlike a town
famous for its wine as a town well could. According to official records
there are 412 acres of vineyard within the city limits, but there is
nothing which could be called a hillside within two miles or more,
and most of the country round about is in sugar-beets or potatoes,

and as flat as a potato pancake. The one celebrated vineyard, which consists of only 26 acres, is in the northern part of the town, and it is easy to miss it if one is traveling by car. This is the "Liebfrauenstift," and it surrounds the Liebfrauenkirche, the Church of Our Lady. In all probability this gave its name to Liebfraumilch, but the wine which it produces is sold as "Liebfrauenstiftswein," not Liebfraumilch, today. The vineyard is divided among three growers, all of them substantial and important, and it certainly produces the best wines which such alluvial soil is capable of yielding under any circumstances. Nevertheless, Liebfrauenstiftswein is no Niersteiner or Nackenheimer; I have tasted far better wines called simply Liebfraumilch than any it has ever produced or is even likely to produce. But such Liebfraumilchs, of course, did not come from Worms. The three producers in question are *Valckenberg, Langenbach,* and *Freiherr Heyl zu Herrnsheim,* and the Liebfrauenstiftswein that carries their labels is authentic—as good as any wine from Worms can be.

Ingelheim, which faces Schloss Johannisberg across the Rhine, is not part of the *Rheinfront* at all, but off in an entirely different direction, west and downstream from Mainz, on the road to Bingen. Reputedly the birthplace of Charlemagne, it still boasts some rather impressive ruins, and the medieval walls of its upper town are picturesque and for the most part intact. Unlike all other wine-producing towns in Rheinhessen, it is decidedly more famous for its red wines, which are very pleasant if undistinguished, than for its whites, which are of no consequence at all. The total acreage is fairly large—some 350 acres producing red wine, and nearly twice as much in Sylvaners and Müller-Thurgaus.

** *Bingen,* directly opposite Rüdesheim, occupies a narrow triangle of flat land, formed by the junction of the Nahe and Rhine, at the extreme northwestern corner of Rheinhessen. Behind it rises the vast red buttress of the Scharlachberg, or "scarlet hill" (although its color is rather dusky brick than scarlet), and a good part of the Scharlachberg, particularly the slope that faces south, and away from Bingen, is covered with vines. These, little known outside Germany, produce some of Hessia's best wines.

Originally, and not too long ago, three separate towns were involved—Bingen itself and Büdesheim and Kempten—but the two latter are now part of what might be called "greater Bingen," and are known as Bingen-Büdesheim and Bingen-Kempten. From the wine-drinker's point of view, all that seems to have been accomplished by this merger is to make a few wine and vineyard names, which were already complicated enough, somewhat longer and more difficult. Not everyone is prepared to ask for a Bingen-Büdesheimer Scharlachberg Spätlese when what he wants is a good bottle of Rhine wine. But the wines, of course, are as good as ever.

The leading producers in Bingen are the *Staatsweingut,* the *Villa Sachsen (Curt Burger's Erben)* and *P. A. Ohler.* And here, some in Bingen-Kempten and some in Bingen-Büdesheim, are the best *Lagen* out of the 720 acres of vineyard:

Binger-Büdesheimer Scharlachberg	Binger Ohligberg
Binger-Büdesheimer Häusling	Binger Mainzerweg
Binger-Büdesheimer Steinkautsweg	Binger Rosengarten
Binger-Büdesheimer Schnackenberg	Binger Schlossberg
Binger-Kempter Rheinberg	Binger Eiselberg
Binger-Kempter Pfarrgarten	Binger Schwätzerchen
Binger-Kempter Kirchberg	Binger Rochusberg

Just for the record, here is a list of the other towns in Hessia which have over 250 acres of vineyard. Those with some claim to superior quality are in italics: Albig, Alzey, *Bechtheim,* Dalsheim, *Dittelsheim,* Dromersheim, Elsheim, Flonheim, Framersheim, *Gau Algesheim,* Gau Bickelheim, Gau Odernheim, Gross Winternheim, *Gundersheim,* Horrweiler, Jugenheim, *Mettenheim,* Nieder-Florsheim, Nieder-Saulheim, *Ockenheim, Osthofen,* St. Johann, Schwabenheim, *Schwabsburg,* Selzen, Siefersheim, Sprendlingen, *Westhofen,* Weinheim, Wöllstein, Zornheim.

VI

THE NAHE

F ORTY years ago, when German wines were at the height of their pre-World War and pre-Prohibition popularity, the wines of the Nahe occupied an honorable and important place among them. This was particularly true in and around St. Louis, where the fact that several of the leading Nahe producers were called Anheuser, and were actually cousins of the Anheusers of Anheuser-Busch and Budweiser fame, gave them an immediate entrée. At the turn of the century no good New York wine list was complete without its Nahe wine listings. Yet today Nahe wines are hardly known in America at all.

It is difficult to explain this eclipse. Nahe wines are certainly much better now than they were in the days of our fathers and grandfathers; as a matter of fact, one of the best vineyards of all (Schloss Böckelheimer Kupfergrube) did not even exist in 1900 and was later created by the German State on a steep hillside originally covered with scrub and brush. Today the wines of the Nahe fully deserve a place alongside those of the Rheinpfalz and the Rheingau, of the Moselle and Hessia. Most of them are made from the Riesling grape, and well made; even the Sylvaners and rare Traminers have considerable distinction and breed, particularly those that come from the precipitous valley upstream and southwest of Bad Kreuznach. They are all shipped in brown bottles like the wines of Hessia, and their nomenclature is rather like that of Hessia, or the Moselle, than like that of the Rheingau: in other words, expressions like *"feine*

Spätlese," "feinste Auslese," etc., are frequently used, whereas the word "Cabinet" is not.

Because of the fact that the Valley of the Nahe lies between that of the Moselle and the Rhine Valley proper, some writers have chosen to say that the wines, too, are midway between the Moselles and Rhines in character. This seems to me a poor way to describe them: their qualities are their own; the best of them are grown on red sandstone soil very different from the slate of the Moselle, and their bouquet, however admirable, is not a Moselle bouquet by any means. It is, as a matter of fact, more like that of a good Niersteiner.

We have had occasion before to mention the mouth of the Nahe—it is directly opposite the Rheingau's Rüdesheimer Berg, and almost in the shadow of the Binger Scharlachberg, the westernmost vineyard of Rheinhessen. Actually four districts—Rheingau, Rheinhessen, the Mittel-Rhein and the Nahe—come together at this point; what are officially classified as the Nahe vineyards begin a little further south, half way between Bingen and Bad Kreuznach.

Despite the fact that it was almost totally destroyed in the War, Bad Kreuznach has become once more an important center of the wine trade, and its celebrated *Seitz-Werke,* which manufactured filters used by vintners all over the world, has been completely rebuilt. With the single exception of the State Domain at Schloss Böckelheim, all of the leading producers are in Kreuznach, and all of them own vineyards in at least three or four different towns. The seven most important are listed below, together with the names of the towns in which they have holdings. It might be added that there are about a dozen large *Winzergenossenschaften* in the Nahe district, which can generally be relied on for wines in the middle and lower price brackets. The seven "great" producers:

Paul Anheuser. Vineyards in Kreuznach, Schloss Böckelheim, Norheim, Niederhausen, Monzingen and Altenbamberg.

Weingut Herf und Engelsmann Erben. Holdings in Kreuznach, Winzenheim, Rotenfels, etc.

Weingut Gutleuthof, Carl Andres. Kreuznach, Roxheim, etc.

Weingut August Anheuser. Vineyards in Kreuznach, Schloss Böckelheim, Niederhausen, etc.

Weingut Graf von Plettenberg. Holdings in Kreuznach, Norheim, Bretzenheim, Winzenheim, etc.

Landes-Weinbaulehranstalt (the Provincial Wine School). Kreuznach, Norheim, Niederhausen, etc.

Verwaltung der Staatl. Weinbaudomanen (the State Domain). Vineyards in Schloss Böckelheim, Niederhausen, Münster, Rotenfels, etc.

Kreuznach is not only the commercial but the geographical center of its district, and in its own right a wine-producing town of absolutely first rank. The nearby villages that belong in the same high category are all further upstream, which here means south, and they are all strung along the narrow, winding Nahe Valley: Münster (or Bad Münster-am-Stein), Norheim, Niederhausen, Schloss Böckelheim, and, in the same direction but of a somewhat lower class, Ebernberg, Altenbamberg and Monzingen.

The rolling hills west and northwest and north of Kreuznach are also for the most part covered with vines, and in this essentially secondary area three or four towns are truly outstanding—Roxheim is certainly the best of them, with Winzenheim and Bretzenheim fairly close behind.

The following is a brief summary of towns and their best-known plots, or *Lagen:*

* *Bretzenheimer*	Vogelsang, Schützenhöll.
*** *Kreuznacher*	Hinkelstein, Kröttenpfuhl, Kahlenberg, Narrenkappe, Forst, Mönchberg, Steinweg, St. Martin, Kronenberg, Mühlenberg, Brücken, Mollenbrunnen, Osterhölle, Brückes-Treppchen.
Monzinger	Gabelstück.
** *Münsterer*	Pittersberg, Dautenpflänzer, Langenberg.
*** *Niederhäuser*	Hermannshöhle, Hermannsberg, Pfingstweide, Steyer, Rosenheck, Rossel, Klamm.
*** *Norheimer*	Kafels, Kirschheck, Götzenfels, Hinterfels, Dellchen.
** *Roxheimer*	Huttenberg, Hollenpfad, Birkenberg, Muhlenberg, Neuenberg.

* *Rüdesheimer*	Rosengarten
*** *Schloss* *Böckelheimer*	Kupfergrube, Kupferberg, Königsfels, Königsberg, In dem Felsen, Mühlberg, Felsenberg, Heimberg.
* *Winzerheimer*	Berg, Rosenheck, Honigberg, Schild.

VII

THE PALATINATE

(Pfalz)

THE Pfalz, or Rheinpfalz, or Palatinate, as it is called in English, is an odd little corner of Germany, full of surprises and contradictions, and full of an odd sort of earthy charm. Few tourists ever see it, tourists being what they are—after all, there *is* a superhighway, an *Autobahn,* on the other bank of the Rhine, on which one can average 80 miles an hour, and there are Baden-Baden and Heidelberg as added attractions. But the Pfalz is eminently worth seeing just the same.

To begin at the very beginning, the Pfalz takes its name, rather deviously and indirectly to be sure, from one of the original seven hills of Rome. The word *Pfalz,* in German, is a variation of *Palast,* or palace, and all three words derive from the "Palatine" Hill, on which the Roman emperors constructed the first of their imperial residences, over two thousand years ago. Eventually, of course, they had their "palaces" in other parts of the Empire as well, and the official charged with the supervision of these became known as the *"comes palatinus,"* or "Count Palatine." The title survived only in Germany, and by 1350 had become hereditary there, with vast estates attached to it, including all of what is now the Pfalz. It is safe to assume that the "Count Palatine" who was one of Portia's unsuccessful suitors in the *Merchant of Venice,* was called *Pfalzgraf* at home, and he may, for all we know, have been a vineyard owner in Deidesheim or Forst.

In any case, hundreds of years before Shakespeare's day, the Pfalz was famous as the "Wine Cellar of the Holy Roman Empire," *propter vini copiam,* on account of the abundance of its wines, and it is still famous for precisely the same reason.

The modern Pfalz is bounded on the south and southwest by France, and on the west by the Territory of the Saar. Being a border province it has seen more than its share of wars, and having been repeatedly invaded and ravaged and burned, especially during the 17th and 18th Centuries, in quarrels that were none of its making, it has largely lost its taste for things military.

For this is a very peaceful and peaceable country, the Pfalz, very like Alsace, almost a northern prolongation of Alsace. The hills of its Haardt range, pine-covered and crowned with innumerable ruined castles, are really a northern extension of the Alsatian Vosges, and the two provinces have much in common—nature has been kind to both. The Pfalz has the warmest climate of Germany, and the lowest annual rainfall. Like Alsace, it is a country of wonderfully prolific orchards, famous not only for their cherries, their peaches and their plums, but even for their apricots and figs and almonds, which at this latitude is rare. Like Alsace, it is a land of plentiful game and trout streams, of old walled villages and half-timber houses, steep roofs and wrought-iron tavern signs and window boxes full of flowers. Both are districts of white wine, of pale, fresh Sylvaners, "spicy" Traminers, and noble Rieslings. Both are districts of copious meals and stout trenchermen. And if there is no cuisine in the Pfalz to equal that of Strasbourg and Colmar and Ammerschwihr, there are no wines in Alsace to equal the best of Wachenheim and Deidesheim and Forst.

The good people of the Pfalz are notoriously fond of their own wines and they drink them plentifully, at all times and in all seasons. First, just after the vintage, in the form of what they call *Federweisser* (or "feather-white"—though it is certainly no beverage for anyone who wears the white feather of a temperance organization); at this stage it is half grape juice and half wine, still a little cloudy, still a little sweet, young and blond and innocent-looking, but as treacherous as a knife in the back. Second, they drink it, all year long and happily and properly as *Schoppenwein,* which means something like *vin de carafe* but sounds a little less elegant. And finally they drink it, when they find it above average quality and worth bottling, as *Flaschenwein,* a year or many years later, on real occasions, with their friends.

Happily, we are never likely to see the explosive *Federweisser* outside of Germany. And we are hardly likely to get much *Schoppen-wein* either, unless it is disguised as one of its betters; all of it is more agreeable when its age can be counted in months, not years; none of it is of really outstanding quality, and if it is called *Schoppen-*

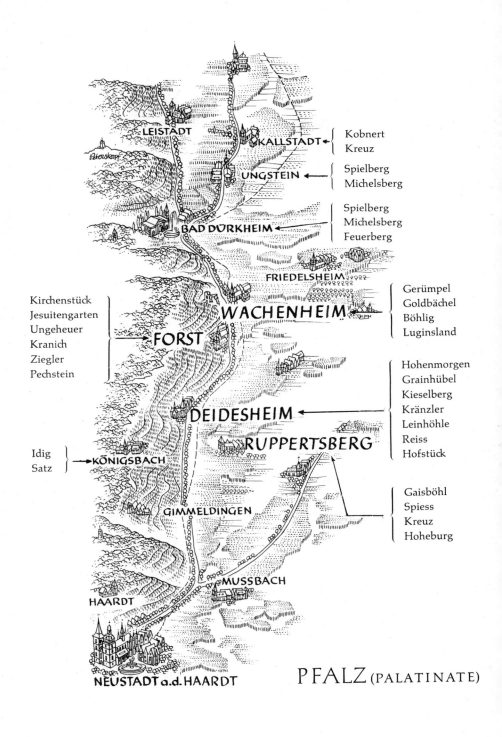

LEISTADT

Peterskopf

KALLSTADT {
Kobnert
Kreuz

UNGSTEIN {
Spielberg
Michelsberg

BAD DÜRKHEIM {
Spielberg
Michelsberg
Feuerberg

FRIEDELSHEIM

Kirchenstück
Jesuitengarten
Ungeheuer
Kranich
Ziegler
Pechstein
}
FORST

WACHENHEIM {
Gerümpel
Goldbächel
Böhlig
Luginsland

DEIDESHEIM {
Hohenmorgen
Grainhübel
Kieselberg
Kränzler
Leinhöhle
Reiss
Hofstück

RUPPERTSBERG

Idig
Satz
} KÖNIGSBACH

{
Gaisböhl
Spiess
Kreuz
Hoheburg

GIMMELDINGEN

MUSSBACH

HAARDT

NEUSTADT a.d. HAARDT

PFALZ (PALATINATE)

wein to begin with, we may be fairly sure that it is better thus than prepared and bottled for the export market.

What we get from the Pfalz, in short, is its cream—the great wines from a few great vineyards and great vintners, about three-quarters of them made from the Riesling grape.

Only about 10% of the Pfalz vineyards, however, are planted to Rieslings. There is an approximately equal acreage of Müller-Thurgau, and the rest—apart from red grape varieties (mostly Portugieser) for red wine—is Sylvaner. It must be admitted that *on hillside vineyards in the central section of the Pfalz*—the "Mittel-Haardt," of which more later—the Sylvaner yields some wines which are very good indeed, clean and light and fine, sound younger brothers to the greater Rieslings. But the vast bulk of the 15,000,000 annual gallons of Pfalz wine comes, not from these slopes, but from the heavy, alluvial soil of the Rhine plain. This is *Schoppenwein* and no mistake about it; it has, especially in good years, an almost indescribable heavy flavor which the Germans call a *Bodengeschmack,* a taste of earth. The French (although I have never run across a French wine with a flavor of this sort as pronounced as it is in the common wines of the Pfalz) call it a *goût de terroir.* I can only say that it is not very agreeable to an educated palate, just as a cheap cigar is not very agreeable to a lover of fine Havana tobacco.

In the better Pfalz wines, the Rieslings especially, there is no trace of this, and these are perhaps the best of all German wines to drink with the best of German food. Considerably fuller in body than the wines of the Moselle, less mild and soft than the wines of Hessia, perhaps less overwhelming in bouquet than the great Rheingaus, they have a remarkable and attractive balance, and they are as easy to drink with food as the fine white Burgundies of France. The *Auslesen* and *Beerenauslesen* are of course another matter—these are dessert wines, and among the most distinguished in the world.

The vineyard district of the Pfalz, like many another great vineyard district, consists essentially of the lower slopes of a single range of hills; like the vineyards of the Burgundian Côte d'Or, they face east over a plain, and are between five and seven hundred feet above sea level. The hills, the *Haardt Gebirge,* run from a thousand to twelve hundred feet higher at their wooded summits, and extend from Herxheim, north of Bad Dürkheim, almost to the French frontier.

At the foot of the hills, threading its way through the vineyards and vineyard towns, running fifty miles from Kleinbockenheim, on the border of Hessia, south to Schweigen, on the French frontier, is a famous road. This, as unlike an *Autobahn* or superhighway as a road well could be, is the *Deutsche Weinstrasse,* the "German Wine Road." It is certainly no route for a person in a hurry, but to a lover of good wine, picturesque villages and enchanting countryside, it would be hard to recommend a more rewarding journey. There are thirty-five little vineyard towns on the road itself, and at least a dozen others, all worth seeing, within two or three miles of it.

Traveling the *Weinstrasse,* it is easy to recognize the three main sections into which the Pfalz vineyards are divided. First, the less steep, rolling country from the Hessian border town to Herxheim; this, the Unter-Haardt, is a country of small and common wines, and need not greatly concern us. Second, the Mittel-Haardt, between Herxheim (or Freinsheim) and Neustadt; this is the district of great wines, the center and kernel of the Pfalz, and we shall have considerably more to say about it in a moment. Third, extending south from Neustadt almost to the French frontier, the Ober-Haardt; this is *Schoppenwein* country, where the major emphasis is on quantity and on yield per acre. In all fairness it should be said that the villages almost make up, in picturesqueness and charm, for the mediocre quality of their wines, and occasionally, too, one runs across a bottle of something that is rather more than passable from Hambach, or St. Martin or Maikammer or Weyher. But it is the Mittel-Haardt and the Mittel-Haardt alone which produces the wines that have made the Pfalz world-famous.

It is eighteen miles from Herxheim to Neustadt, and the vineyards run like a green ribbon, a mile to two miles wide, between the dark pine forests above and the flat farmland below. Including both Herxheim and Neustadt, there are seventeen villages in all in this section of *Edelweine;* nine of the seventeen produce wines that are better than those of the Ober-Haardt, but not much better, and you will rarely see their names—Herxheim, Freinsheim, Leistadt, Friedelsheim, Niederkirchen, Mussbach, Gimmeldingen, Haardt and Neustadt—on labels of wine bottled for the export market. Four others—Kallstadt, Ungstein, Bad Dürkheim and Königsbach—produce wines that are excellent and in rare instances great. The last four, in the exact middle of the Mittel-Haardt, are the incomparable ones—from north to south, Wachenheim, Forst, Deidesheim, Ruppertsberg.

From Wachenheim to Ruppertsberg it is only about five miles, even by way of the curving *Weinstrasse,* and some four square miles of vines—roughly 2500 acres—are alone responsible for the *Spitzen-weine,* or "peak" wines of the Pfalz.

These 2500 precious acres are divided and sub-divided and classified to an extent which is hardly believable. In the four townships there are at least 250 vineyard sites, or *Lagen,* each one with its well-known, well-established name, and its legal boundaries. The largest can hardly consist of over thirty acres and there are certainly not more than a dozen of the 250 which are the property of a single owner. Some fourteen producers have vines in that small, extraordinary parcel called Forster Ungeheuer, for example, and it is therefore possible to buy authentic and estate-bottled Forster Ungeheuer under fourteen or more different labels. And they will be fourteen quite different wines—some, quite possibly, made from grapes picked early and others from grapes picked late; they will have been pressed and fermented and aged in fourteen different cellars according to the ideas of fourteen different cellar-masters, and bottled under wholly dissimilar conditions and at different times. In order to buy Pfalz wines intelligently, it is essential, therefore, to be familiar not only with the town names and the vineyard names, but with the producers' names as well. Fortunately, this is not as difficult as it sounds. Most of the really small producers have banded themselves together into cooperatives—*Winzervereine* or *Winzergenossenschaften*—and offer their better wines under the cooperative label. Apart from these, there are eight and only eight "major" producers, whose holdings in Wachenheim, Forst, Deidesheim and Ruppertsberg amount to twenty-five acres or more, who produce, in other words, over 5000 cases of wine a year. Nine others own between ten and twenty-five acres (2000 to 5000 cases a year), and those who produce less than 2000 cases need hardly concern us here.

The seventeen, listed alphabetically, are as follows (the first three, the largest, are known as "the three B's"):

Geheimer Rat Dr. v. Bassermann-Jordan	90 acres in Deidesheim, Forst Ruppertsberg, Bad Dürkheim and Ungstein.
Dr. Bürklin-Wolf	159 acres in Wachenheim, Forst, Deidesheim, Ruppertsberg and Bad Dürkheim.
Reichsrat v. Buhl	192 acres in Deidesheim, Forst, Wachenheim, Ruppertsberg and Königsbach.
Dr. Deinhard	60 acres in Deidesheim, Forst, Wachenheim and Ruppertsberg.

Hch. Koch-Herzog Erben	28 acres in Deidesheim, Ruppertsberg and Forst.
Dr. med. Jos. Pioth	36 acres in Deidesheim and Forst.
Georg Siben Erben	29 acres in Deidesheim, Forst and Ruppertsberg.
Wilhelm Spindler	43 acres in Forst, Deidesheim, Ruppertsberg and Wachenheim.

Josef Biffar
Dietz-Matti
Herbert Giessen Erben
Ferd. Heinemann
Dr. Kern
Jul. Ferd. Kimich
Jos. Reinhardt II
Heinrich Spindler
A. Tiemann

Producers owning between 10 and 25 acres in the four great vineyard towns.

It should not be imagined that these estates consist of large holdings or of entire vineyards. With a very few exceptions (of which Forster Jesuitengarten is much the most important) ALL of the better vineyards of the Pfalz are divided among a number of different owners, and the acreages given above, far from representing unbroken areas of vineyard, are made up, literally, of scores of tiny portions of different *Lagen,* often of an acre or less, and often four or five miles from one another. Thus the famous Bassermann-Jordan family, in addition to Forster Jesuitengarten, owns portions of over twenty different *Lagen* in Deidesheim, of fifteen in Forst, and over a dozen in Ruppertsberg. Dr. Bürklin-Wolf is the sole owner of several Wachenheim vineyards (Rechbächel, Langebächel, etc.) but has holdings in more than twenty others, and some of the producers with only ten acres in all will actually make twenty different wines from twenty different vineyards in three or four different townships. These, of course, are never blended but are scrupulously kept separate, and it is hardly surprising that the quantity of wine available of a given vineyard, producer and year, is in almost all cases extremely limited, and often amounts to no more than a single cask of 250 gallons. This, from a commercial viewpoint, may seem hardly sensible, but there is an old adage about the proof of the pudding, and it is hard to imagine how the great Pfalz wines could be any better than they are.

Needless to say, there is an enormous amount of Pfalz wine produced and sold and even exported which is not handled in this way at all. It goes in barrel, not long after the vintage, from the producer to one of the many shippers in Neustadt or Bad Dürkheim, or even Worms or Mainz. There, if it is a Deidesheimer Hofstück, for example, it will be blended with other Deidesheimer Hofstücks, from other growers, to make 2500 gallons rather than 250 of a single wine. Or, if its origin is less distinguished, it may be sold simply as Deidesheimer, with the shipper's brand or name. It is certainly a mistake to suppose that such wines are necessarily inferior to unblended estate-bottlings, for this is not by any means the case, whatever the purists may say. A shipper's wine may be magnificent, or may be worthless, but wine merchants, by and large, are as honest as other people, and a shipper who makes a practice of selling bad wine is not often successful in the long run. On the other hand, what is true in Germany as a whole is true no less in the Pfalz; almost all of the best vineyards are owned by producers who bottle their own wines, and if they sell part of their production in bulk and part in bottle, it is safe to assume that the best goes to market under their own name and under their own label. This may mean, and generally does, more trouble for the consumer, who cannot be sure of getting a continuing supply of a wine he likes, and who has to work his way through all the complexities of vineyard names, producers' names and the like. But the game is worth the candle.

It would be too bad to conclude even a brief chapter such as this without at least a word about the innumerable wine-and-vintage-festivals of the Pfalz. The Pfälzer love their wines, and they are never happier than when they can find an excuse for opening a few special bottles for friends or appreciative guests. Over a hundred thousand visitors usually attend the so-called *"Wurstmarkt,"* or "sausage sale" in Bad Dürkheim, in September, which has a great deal more to do with wine than with sausages, and when the Wine Queen of the Pfalz is crowned in Neustadt in October, the whole Palatinate is there. But there are literally dozens of others, since nearly every village has its *Feste,* and they run from Whitsuntide through all the good weather until after the vintage.

THE PALATINATE VINEYARDS

The following is a rather more detailed summary of the major Pfalz vineyards and their wines, as one encounters them traveling south along the *Weinstrasse,* from Kleinbockenheim, on the border of Hessia, to Schweigen, and the French frontier:

The Unter-Haardt

This, the northern third of the Pfalz, produces little or nothing in the way of wine fit for bottling and export. The only possible exception is one wine produced, largely from Gewürztraminer grapes, along the Hessian border in the two villages of Zell (which should not be confused with Zell, on the Moselle) and Harxheim (which should not be confused with Herxheim, near Bad Dürkheim). This goes to market under the extraordinary name of Zeller Schwarzer Herrgott, no doubt to compete with the Moselle's Zeller Schwarze Katz. It is not very distinguished.

The Mittel-Haardt

The seventeen villages and towns of this central section of the Pfalz are listed below, together with their better-known producers and *Lagen.* Asterisks have been used as indications of superior quality, but any such ratings are only generalizations at best, and I have tasted (though not often) exceedingly poor wines from villages to which I have given three asterisks (***) such as Deidesheim, and also (though not often) excellent wines from villages to which I have given no asterisks at all.

Although only about one-tenth of the Pfalz's great acreage of vines is in Rieslings, you will find little else planted in the best *Lagen,* and in general the towns where the Riesling predominates, or at least runs well over the 10% average, are those that produce the best wine. For this reason I have given the percentage of Rieslings in each one of the seventeen towns.

The Pfalz also produces over half of all the red wine of Germany, but a good deal of this is drunk by the *Winzer* themselves, or sold locally as *Schoppenwein,* as it properly should be. The best of it, compared to the fairly good wines of France, is poor stuff indeed.

Here then is a brief roster of what has made the Pfalz famous:

Herxheim. *(About 375 acres.) 15% Rieslings. Considerable red wine.* The northern limit of the Mittel-Haardt, but quality-wise of not much consequence. The *Winzergenossenschaft,* or vintners' cooperative, is by all odds the largest producer.

Leistadt. (450 acres.) 10% Rieslings. Considerable red wine. Mediocre.

Freinsheim. (Some 590 acres.) 10% Rieslings. Considerable red wine. Another village of secondary quality although an extremely picturesque one. *Lehmann-Hilgard* and the *Winzerverein* are major producers, and the better *Lagen* include:

Freinsheimer Gottesacker	Freinsheimer Satzen
Freinsheimer Gross	Freinsheimer Oschelkopf

* Kallstadt. (Some 720 acres.) 40% Rieslings. Considerable red wine. While by no means of first rank, Kallstadt has a number of hillside vineyards which produce honorable and even excellent Rieslings and Sylvaners. Dependable bottlers include *Stumpf-Fitz,* several members of a family named *Ruprecht,* the *Winzergenossenschaft* and the *Winzerverein.* Note:

Kallstadter Kobnert	Kallstadter Kreuz
Kallstadter Steinacker	Kallstadter Nill
Kallstadter Kronenberg	Kallstadter Annaberg
Kallstadter Saumagen	Kallstadter Horn

* Ungstein. (About 650 acres.) 19% Rieslings. Considerable red wine. Another town of sound and creditable wines. *Fitz-Ritter, Bassermann-Jordan* (see under Deidesheim, farther on), the *Winzerverein* and the *Winzergenossenschaft* are major bottlers, although the two latter produce more red wine than white. The best vineyards:

Ungsteiner Spielberg	Ungsteiner Michelsberg
Ungsteiner Herrenberg	Ungsteiner Roterd

* Bad Dürkheim. (Over 1900 acres.) About 15% Rieslings. Substantial amount of red wine which, although locally regarded as magnificent, is frankly undistinguished, being made from the inferior Portugieser grape. Nestling among its vineyards, at the foot of the forest-covered hills of the Haardt, with mineral springs,

many hotels, and even a gambling casino, Bad Dürkheim is a popular resort town, and a very pretty one. Among its minor attractions is the so-called "Dürkheimer Fass" ("Wine-Vat"), a restaurant in the form of a barrel—which could, theoretically, hold half of Dürkheim's annual wine production. This production, incidentally, is very large, for Dürkheim is by a considerable margin the largest wine-producing town in all Germany. The white wines from its better vineyards, while rarely of the highest class, are good and widely known, and deserve their reputation. Leading producers include *Fitz-Ritter* and *Stumpf-Fitz, Bassermann-Jordan* and *Bürklin-Wolf,* the *Winzergenossenschaft* and the *Winzerverein.* And the best *Lagen* are:

Dürkheimer Michelsberg	Dürkheimer Spielberg
Dürkheimer Hochbenn	Dürkheimer Schenkenböhl
Dürkheimer Fuchsmantel	Dürkheimer Feuerberg

** *Wachenheim. (840 acres.) About 25% Rieslings. A little red wine.* Northernmost of the four great wine-producing villages of the Pfalz, and directly adjoining Forst, the most highly rated of all, Wachenheim has at least a dozen vineyards that have acquired international fame. The best Wachenheimers of great years are among the most sought-after wines of Germany, for they combine great body and bouquet with extraordinary finesse. Dr. Bürklin-Wolf, the most active present figure in Palatinate wine affairs, is the leading producer; his 160 acres of vineyard include substantial portions of ten out of the twelve Wachenheimer *Lagen* listed below, plus of course important holdings in Forst, Deidesheim, Ruppertsberg and Bad Dürkheim. Similarly, excellent Wachenheimers are produced and bottled by *von Buhl, Dr. Deinhard, Spindler,* etc., who have their establishments in Deidesheim and Forst. The two growers' cooperatives, the *Winzerverein Luginsland,* and the *Winzergenossenschaft Wachtenburg,* are among the oldest and best equipped of Germany. The top vineyards are:

Wachenheimer Gerümpel	Wachenheimer Goldbächel
Wachenheimer Böhlig	Wachenheimer Wolfsdarm
Wachenheimer Bächel	Wachenheimer Luginsland
Wachenheimer Rechbächel	Wachenheimer Langebächel
Wachenheimer Altenburg	Wachenheimer Hägel
Wachenheimer Dreispitz	Wachenheimer Schenkenböhl

Friedelsheim. (360 acres.) 10% Rieslings. Considerable red wine.
Directly east of Wachenheim, on the edge of the
plain. Rather common wines. *Karl Köster* is an important producer,
and there is a *Winzerverein.*

*** *Forst.* *(495 acres.) 70% Rieslings. No red wine.* Although it
has less than 800 inhabitants and a single street
(which appropriately enough, is the so-called *Deutsche Weinstrasse*),
Forst is one of the most famous wine-producing towns of the world.
Through its high, arched doorways of red sandstone you can get a
glimpse of prosperous-looking, flower-grown, shady courtyards, and
of the press-houses to which the grapes are brought in autumn. Everywhere else—around the church, in the very back yards of the village
buildings—there are vines. This is hardly surprising, since many of
the best vineyard plots of Forst are practically in the village itself,
and since two of them, Jesuitengarten and Kirchenstück, are rated
about the most valuable agricultural land in Germany.

The extraordinary quality and bouquet of the Forster wines is
said in large part to be due to certain extraordinary outcroppings of
black basalt which exist in the vineyards of Forst, but not elsewhere
in the Pfalz nor, to my knowledge, elsewhere in Germany. There are
quarries above and behind the vineyards, and the better wine-producers regularly buy the rubble from these quarries, and spread it
among their vines, not only in Forst, but in Deidesheim and Ruppertsberg and Wachenheim as well, for the results that it gives are reputedly
remarkable, almost in the nature of a miraculous blood-transfusion
which confers on the favored vineyards the ability to produce wines
with the Forster elegance and the Forster *blume.*

All of the "great" wine producers of the Pfalz have holdings in
Forst, even if their homes and principal cellars are in Wachenheim
or Deidesheim, and you will see their names and labels on "Forster"
wine. These great producers include: *Reichsrat von Buhl, Dr. von
Bassermann-Jordan, Dr. Bürklin-Wolf, Dr. Deinhard, Dr. Pioth, Wilhelm Spindler, Heinrich Spindler;* less important but equally reputable
are *Dercum, Heinemann, Kern, Kimich, Magin Erben, Mosbacher
Erben, Wallbillich, Werle Erben,* and *Wiss.* The *Forster Winzerverein*
also enjoys a good reputation. There are more than fifty officially
listed vineyards—of these, the following are generally considered the
best, in more or less this order:

Forster Kirchenstück	Forster Jesuitengarten
Forster Ungeheuer	Forster Ziegler
Forster Kranich	Forster Freundstück
Forster Langenmorgen	Forster Langenacker
Forster Pechstein	Forster Mühlweg
Forster Elster	Forster Hellholz
Forster Langenböhl	Forster Fleckinger
Forster Trift	Forster Walshöhle
Forster Sechsmorgen	Forster Gerling
Forster Musenhang	Forster Alser
Forster Pfeiffer	Forster Boländer

*** *Deidesheim.* *(960 acres.) 60% Rieslings. Insignificant amount of red wine.* Fourth in total vineyard area among the wine towns of the Pfalz (and of Germany), Deidesheim is easily first in the production of great wine—in quality it is on a par with Forst, and there is no higher praise possible. The little town itself is extraordinarily charming too, with old patrician homes built out of red sandstone, a lovely, ancient *Rathaus,* or Town Hall, a score, at least, of winding, narrow streets and alleyways, picturesque and full of the flavor of the past, and gardens green with figs and apricots and vines. Although less important than Bad Dürkheim as far as the general wine trade is concerned, it is the undisputed fine wine center of the Pfalz, and the home of all of the really great producers except Bürklin-Wolf (Wachenheim) and Spindler (Forst). These "great producers" include, of course, first of all, the heirs of the late dean of German wine growers, *Dr. Friedrich von Bassermann-Jordan,* who was honorary president of almost every Palatinate wine organization and author of many erudite volumes on the history of the vine, whose museum of antiquities and library of books and bottles are world famous and who was the sole owner of Forster Jesuitengarten; second, *Reichsrat von Buhl,* whose cellars stretch for a whole kilometer under the town, and whose 190 acres of vineyard constitute the largest privately owned domain in Germany; third, a half dozen others, less large perhaps but of no less impeccable reputation: *Biffar, Dr. Deinhard, Koch-Herzog Erben, Jos. Reinhardt, Dr. Pioth, Siben Erben.* It should of course also be kept in mind that several producers listed under Wachenheim and Forst, above, have important holdings in Deidesheim as well—*Bürklin-Wolf,* particularly. The *Winzerverein* and *Winzergenossenschaft* in Deidesheim rank as major cooperatives, and good smaller producers include: *Dercum, Dietz-Matti, Giessen Erben, Dr. Haberer, Dr. Kern, Kimich, Kramer, Mosbacher Erben,* the *Pfarrweingut, Arnold Siben* and *Tiemann.* The following vineyards are generally considered the best, and in approximately this order:

Deidesheimer Hohenmorgen	Deidesheimer Grainhübel
Deidesheimer Kieselberg	Deidesheimer Kränzler
Deidesheimer Leinhöhle	Deidesheimer Rennpfad
Deidesheimer Geheu	Deidesheimer Kalkofen
Deidesheimer Grain	Deidesheimer Reiss
Deidesheimer Mühle	Deidesheimer Dopp
Deidesheimer Herrgottsacker	Deidesheimer Langenmorgen
Deidesheimer Forster Strasse	Deidesheimer Mäushöhle
Deidesheimer Hahnenböhl	Deidesheimer Fleckinger
Deidesheimer Weinbach	Deidesheimer Hofstück

Niederkirchen. (385 acres.) 30% Rieslings. Considerable red wine.
Originally part of Deidesheim, which it adjoins on the east, Niederkirchen produces some fairly good wines—most of these are legally entitled to the name Deidesheimer, and are so marketed. There is an important *Winzerverein,* with holdings in Deidesheim, Forst and Ruppertsberg as well.

** *Ruppertsberg. (420 acres.) About 20% Rieslings. Considerable red wine.* Only about a half mile from Deidesheim, its vineyards forming part of the same incomparable slope, Ruppertsberg is another one of the Palatinate's great names. For all its reputed Roman origin, the village is a great deal less interesting than its wines, and the more important vineyard owners, without exception, live elsewhere—mostly in Deidesheim and Wachenheim. This in no way detracts from the admirable quality of Ruppertsberg's wines and any of the following names on a bottle of Ruppertsberger can be considered a virtual guarantee of superior quality: *Bassermann-Jordan, Bürklin-Wolf, von Buhl, Dr. Deinhard, Dietz-Matti, Jos. Reinhardt, Siben Erben, Wilhelm Spindler.* Ruppertsberg has also an important *Winzerverein* and *Winzergenossenschaft.* The better *Lagen* are, in more or less this order:

Ruppertsberger Gaisböhl	Ruppertsberger Spiess
Ruppertsberger Kreuz	Ruppertsberger Nussbien

Ruppertsberger Reiterpfad	Ruppertsberger Hoheburg
Ruppertsberger Hofstück	Ruppertsberger Goldschmied
Ruppertsberger Achtmorgen	Ruppertsberger Mandelacker
Ruppertsberger Weisslich	Ruppertsberger Kieselberg
Ruppertsberger Linsenbusch	Ruppertsberger Grund

* *Königsbach.* *(325 acres.) 30% Rieslings. Considerable red wine.*
Although a great deal less famous than Ruppertsberg, Königsbach produces wines that are quite in the class with those of its illustrious neighbor. The village is west of the *Weinstrasse* on the edge of the woods—above, rather than below its vineyards. *Reichsrat von Buhl* (see Deidesheim) is the major producer, but there is a large *Winzerverein* and a *Winzergenossenschaft.* The best *Lagen* are:

Königsbacher Idig	Königsbacher Satz
Königsbacher Rolandsberg	Königsbacher Harle
Königsbacher Reiterpfad	Königsbacher Bender
Königsbacher Oelberg	Königsbacher Weissmauer

Gimmeldingen. *(385 acres.) 25% Rieslings. Considerable red wine.*
Perhaps more celebrated for its almonds than for its wines, Gimmeldingen is a pretty little village with a few good vineyards. *Mugler* is a dependable producer, and there is a *Winzergenossenschaft.* Note:

Gimmeldinger Meerspinne   Gimmeldinger Kieselberg

Mussbach. *(915 acres.) 15% Rieslings. Some red wine.* More important for quantity than for quality. A few passable wines.

Haardt. *(360 acres.) 30% Rieslings. A little red wine.* An attractive village, set well back in the sheltering hills, and something of a resort. Wines of no great interest.

Neustadt. *(Some 500 acres.) 25% Rieslings. Considerable red wine.*
A major center of the wine trade, Neustadt is a substantial town, with over 30,000 inhabitants. Wines of secondary quality.

The Ober-Haardt

Between Neustadt and the French border there are over a hundred villages that produce wine, but most of this goes nameless to market and is never bottled. It is mass-produced, and its quality is about what might be expected. Some eight or nine villages occasionally produce something a little better than *Konsumwein* or *Schoppenwein,* and these of course are the hillside villages rather than those down on the plain: Hambach, Maikammer, St. Martin, Rhodt, Weyer, Burrweiler.

VIII

FRANCONIA

(Franken)

THE lovers of Frankenwein, or, as some are pleased to call it, not always accurately, Steinwein, or Steinwein-in-Bocksbeutel, have made almost a cult of their devotion to their special favorites among these wines of the Main Valley. They are quick to point out that Goethe, who drank German wines with great gusto and rather copiously all his life, preferred the wines of Franconia to all others; they are immensely proud of the picturesque Bocksbeutel (which should never be spelled "Boxbeutel"), in which these wines are shipped; they have listed and classified several hundred individual vineyard plots, or *Lagen,* in over a hundred and sixty wine-producing towns, and are ready to do battle at the drop of a hat, or the pop of a cork, over the relative merits of Escherndorfer Lump and Randersackerer Teufelskeller, of Iphöfer Julius-Echter-Berg and the Riesling-vom-Reuschberg from Hörstein.

I must admit that I cannot altogether share this boundless enthusiasm for wines which are almost always agreeable but hardly ever great, nor can I explain Goethe's preference for them except to say that they go very well with food, have a less pronounced bouquet and character than other German wines, are generally quite full-bodied and dry without being tart, and possibly taste more like Alsatian wines or white Burgundies than like Moselles and Rheingaus.

The Franconian vineyards are almost all strung along the valley of the Main, upstream and well east of Mainz and Hochheim and Frankfurt. Between Aschaffenburg and Schweinfurt the river describes a sort of gigantic "W" as it cuts its way through the hills, and here, as on the Moselle, the slopes planted to vineyard are almost exclusively those that face south.

The principal center of the wine trade is Würzburg, the rather handsome, old provincial capital, which has at last recovered from the devastating bombings it underwent during the War. Oddly enough, and alone among all the vineyard towns that I know or have ever heard of, it is as celebrated for its beer as for its wine—Würzburger Edelbrau is highly regarded by experts the world over, and a stein of Würzburger (which is beer) can be quite as pleasant as a Würzburger Stein (which is wine). The first "stein," of course, is a "stone" or earthenware drinking-vessel; the second is Franconia's best vineyard.

As such, the Würzburger Stein has given its name to a sort of generic term (*Steinwein*) often used and wrongly used for Franconian wines as a whole. Correctly speaking, a Steinwein is a wine (and no other) from certain portions of an extraordinary rocky hill within the municipal limits of Würzburg. In any case, no other wine should be so labeled, or could legally be so labeled in Germany.

Since we seem to be embarked on the perilous seas of nomenclature, there are perhaps a few other points which can be cleared up as well. First is the matter of grape varieties. It has long been not only fashionable but legal to call the Sylvaner the "Franken Riesling" in California, and of late it has become permissible to call it simply "Riesling," so that the true, the one, the only Riesling cannot be found except under the name "Johannisberg Riesling." Now the truth is that Sylvaner is sometimes spelled Silvaner and sometimes called the *"Franken Traube"* (or Franconian grape) in Franconia, but, except as a joke, or by the ignorant, it is never called the "Franken Riesling." In the special climate of the Main Valley, where early autumn frosts are the rule rather than the exception, the Sylvaner yields on the whole at least as good and possibly better wine than the Riesling itself, which succeeds only in rare, great years of warm autumn weather. There exist also two crosses of Riesling x Sylvaner; these, although they have the same parents, are quite different, like the children in most cases from any marriage; one is the well-known Müller-Thurgau, cultivated also in Hessia and the Pfalz—the other goes by the rather unfortunate and confusing name of *Mainriesling,* after its river and one, obviously the more famous one, of its ancestors. This is a fairly recent cross and on the basis of present evidence a very promising one. It is a name that we can expect to see in the future on Frankenwein labels, and we may at least hope, although perhaps vainly, that it will continue to be called *Mainriesling,* and not drop the first syllable of its name.

A second point concerns the Franconian bottle, or flagon. This is roughly the shape of an army canteen with a rather long neck, which is perhaps an unfortunate way to describe it, for it is both attractive and picturesque. It is called a *Bocksbeutel* (*Bock* means goat) on account of its fancied resemblance to a goat's scrotum, and it has been so called since time immemorial. The spelling *Boxbeutel* is acceptable only to the etymologically ignorant and the very prudish.

The Bocksbeutel is widely used only for the wines of Franconia, and in other countries, notably Chile, for supposedly similar wines. However it is no less traditional in one other district of Southern Germany, the Mauerwein country near Baden-Baden. A few words about these and other wines of Baden will be found in a succeeding chapter.

In the most recent Yearbook of the *Fränkischer Weinbauverband,* the Franconian Wine Association, 165 vineyard towns are listed, of which 71 admittedly have less than twelve acres under vines. Some seventy-five others have less than fifty acres each and are interesting only to the local *Feinschmeker* and other habitués of the village pubs. Rather more than a dozen town names and perhaps twice that many vineyard names are worth remembering: the major ones are listed below, with asterisks giving at least an idea of average quality.

It should be kept in mind that because of its rather different climate Franconia does not always follow the ratings on vintage charts that are accurate for the Rhine and Moselle. 1952 was at least as good a year as 1953, for example, and 1950 distinctly better than 1949. For the same reason, Spätlesen, Auslesen, and Beerenauslesen are even less common than they are elsewhere, and it has been my experience that they are usually not worth the very high price which, as great rarities, they generally command. *Frankenweine,* outside of Germany, still have the considerable virtue of being fairly inexpensive, and they are excellent values if one does not expect too much of them.

The few really important Franconian producers include, as usual, the German State, but two venerable charitable institutions, the

Juliusspital and the *Burgerspital zum Heiligen Geist,* are even more celebrated, and there are several estates still belonging to old titled families. Here is a list:

Major producers of great reputation:

Juliusspital	Würzburg
Staatsweingut (Hofkellerei)	Würzburg
Burgerspital zum Heiligen Geist	Würzburg
Bayerische Landesanstalt	Veitshochheim
Schloss Saaleck	Hammelburg
Fürstlich Castell'sches Domanenamt	Castell
Fürstlich Löwenstein-Wertheim-	
Rosenberg'sches Weingut	Kreuzwertheim
Fürstlich Löwenstein-Wertheim-	
Freudenberg'sche Hofkelleri	Wertheim

Other dependable producers: (outside of Winzergenossenschaften, of which there are many):

Weingut Johann Ruck	Iphofen
Weingut Bruno Schmitt	Randersacker
Weingut Paul Schmitt	Randersacker
W. Leiniger	Eibelstadt
Weingut Peter Otto Meintzinger	Frickenhausen
Weingut Ernst Gebhardt	Sommerhausen

Here, in alphabetical order, are fifteen of the best wine-producing towns and the vineyard or *Lage* names where they are of interest or consequence:

* *CASTELL (40 acres)* Schlossberg.

** *ESCHERNDORF (195 acres)* Lump, Eulengrube, Hengstberg, Kirchberg.

FRICKENHAUSEN (120 acres) Kapellenberg.

HOMBURG (40 acres) Kallmuth.

HOERSTEIN (60 acres) "Riesling-vom-Reuschberg."

** *IPHOFEN (310 acres)* Julius-Echter-Berg, Kronsberg, Kammer, Burgweg, Kalb.

KLINGENBERG (*35 acres*—mostly red wine).

NORDHEIM (310 acres) Vögelein.

** *RANDERSACKER (390 acres)* Pfülben, Hohbug, Teufelskeller, Spielberg, Marsberg.

** *ROEDELSEE (120 acres)* Kuchenmeister, Schwanleite, Schlossberg.

* *SCHLOSS SAALECK* Schlossberg.

SOMMERACH (170 acres) Katzenkopf.

* *VEITSHOECHHEIM (115 acres)* Neuberg, Abtsberg, Fachtel, Wölflein.

VOLKACH (85 acres) Ratsherr.

*** *WUERZBURG (520 acres)* Stein, Aussere Leiste, Innere Leiste, Neuberg, Abstleite, Harfe, Ständerbühl, Schalksberg, Steinmantel.

IX

THE LESSER DISTRICTS

(Bodensee, Baden, Württemberg, Mittel-Rhein, Ahr)

THIS necessarily must be something of a catch-all chapter, an examination of the diverse and interesting little fellows left in the bottom of our net, now that the really big fish have been taken out and examined separately. Most of these lesser specimens have never been shipped out of Germany and probably never will be; they include wines from the northernmost vineyards of Europe, in the Ahr Valley, near Bonn, and from the southernmost vineyards of Germany, on the banks of Lake Constance. Some of them are never exported because they are not worth exporting; others enjoy and merit a local popularity but would find themselves badly overmatched if forced to compete abroad with somewhat similar wines from sunnier countries; still others are truly excellent but made in such limited quantities that they are promptly drunk up by the producers themselves and their thirsty friends. There is hardly what might be called a "commercial wine" in the whole collection, but perhaps they are all the more interesting for that very reason, and if we are unlikely to see them in the United States, we may at least all hope to taste them, sooner or later, in Germany.

I shall attempt to deal briefly here with the wines of five quite separate and different districts, working downstream from where the Rhine first touches German soil within sight of Switzerland, to where it enters the vast, flat, North European plain toward Holland and the North Sea. Simply defined, the five lesser districts are as follows: 1. The northern shores of Lake Constance; 2. Baden—the whole right bank of the Rhine from Basel, where France and Germany and Switzerland come together, north to Baden-Baden; 3. Württemberg— the upper valley of the Neckar between Stuttgart and Heilbronn; 4. the Mittel-Rhein, north and downstream from the Rheingau, between Lorch and Coblenz; 5. the valley of the Ahr, a small tributary which joins the Rhine near Bonn.

1.   Lake Constance—the Bodensee

Those two great rivers of Western Europe, the Rhône and Rhine, have much in common besides four out of five letters of their name. Both rise in Switzerland; both, just as they leave Switzerland, traverse lakes (Geneva and Constance, respectively) and along the northern shore of both lakes, vines are grown. Neither in quality nor quantity can the wines of Lake Constance, which the Germans call the *Bodensee,* compare with those of Lake Geneva (although the latter could hardly be called great), but some of them are very agreeable nonetheless, especially when drunk on a lakeside terrace when the *Föhn,* the warm south wind, is blowing.

These *Seeweine,* literally "Lake wines," are produced in about a dozen villages dotted along the lake round Meersburg, but only two of these, Meersburg itself and Hagnau, have as much as fifty acres of vines. The Ruländer, or Pinot Gris, of Hagnau is highly regarded, but the most interesting and the typical wine of the Bodensee is an oddity called *Weissherbst,* made from the Spätburgunder, or Pinot Noir. This is what the French would call a *blanc de noirs,* a white wine from black grapes, although here it is sometimes faintly tinged with pink, or what our grandfathers described as "partridge-eye." It is attractive and unusual, but to tell the truth hardly merits the great respect and esteem in which it is held by the local wine-lovers.

2.   Baden

It is not easy to "deal briefly" with Baden, for this province, which comprises a good portion of south-western Germany and faces Alsace across the broad, fertile Rhine valley, produces an astonishingly diverse collection of wines; the most authoritative recent book in German on the subject[1] is one of 757 closely-printed pages and I have heard even this described as "inadequate" by growers who felt that their own vineyard and their own wines had not been discussed in sufficient detail and at sufficient length. I hesitate to think what they will say if this minuscule opus of mine ever falls into their hands.

The two principal towns of Baden are two of the most agreeable small cities in Europe; both are built where the foothills of the Black Forest come down to meet the Rhine plain. Freiburg, with its exquisite Gothic cathedral, is less than forty miles from Switzerland and less than twenty miles from France; the charming resort of Baden-Baden is seventy miles further north, downstream, on the road to Karlsruhe and Heidelberg. This is fertile, hospitable and very lovely country, a sort of German counterpart of Alsace across the way; its hills are covered with orchards as well as vines and behind them the 4000-foot, pine-covered summits of the Schwarzwald rise to form an incomparable background.

Most *Badische* wines are grown along these same Black Forest foothills. One major wine-producing district, *Markgräflerland,* is south of Freiburg, two others are in what is called the *Ortenau,* between Freiburg and Baden-Baden; the fourth and possibly the best, consists of the *Kaiserstuhl,* an extraordinary volcanic "island" which rises like a gigantic mushroom out of the flat river land between Freiburg and the Rhine.

Just as the Riesling is the vine of the Moselle and Rheingau, so the Gutedel is the vine of Markgräflerland, grown to the virtual exclusion of all else; unfortunately, it is no Riesling. It is, in fact, the very productive, rather common grape known as the Chasselas in Alsace and as the Fendant in Switzerland, where it is possibly at its best. Nevertheless, drunk as they should be, when they are young and fresh and, I may add, inexpensive, the Markgräflers from the better vineyard towns can be very pleasant—they are light, mild wines, without much character, it is true, but without that objectionable commonness and *Bodenton* to be found in the cheap wines of the Pfalz. The better vineyard towns, all south of Freiburg, include: Auggen, Ballrechten-Dottingen, Britzingen, Ebringen, Efringen-Kirchen, Ehrenstetten, Kirchhofen, Laufen, Mullheim, Schallstadt, Schliengen and Wolfenweiler.

The wines of the Kaiserstuhl belong in a quite different and considerably higher category although here, too, the Riesling plays

---

[1] *Das Weinbuch von Baden-Wurttemberg.* Sudwestdeutsche Verlagsanstalt, Mannheim, 1954.

an altogether secondary role. There are important plantings of Sylvaner and Müller-Thurgau, of Traminer or Gewürztraminer, and even of Spätburgunder (Pinot Noir) used for the making of red wine. But the predominant variety of the Kaiserstuhl is the Ruländer, the Pinot Gris, and an idea of its potential quality can be gained from the fact that Ruländer Trockenbeerenauslese of a good vintage was sold at auction in Wiesbaden not long ago for 35 Marks (nearly $9) a bottle. This, I hastened to add, was a wine so extraordinary as to be almost in the nature of a freak, but if any of these "lesser" wines of Germany are ever to find a welcome and a ready market overseas, I strongly suspect that it will be the Ruländers from the Kaiserstuhl. They are quite in a class with the best Alsatians, more or less comparable in price, and produced in sufficient quantities to be commercially interesting. We may therefore, one of these days, expect to see such names as Ihringer Winklerberg, Ihringer Blakenhornsberg and Endinger Steingrube on our wine lists. There are some fifteen towns with over 200 acres under vines, and at least as many other smaller ones. Worth noting are: Achkarren, Bechlingen, Bickensohl, Bischoffingen, Bötzingen, Eichstetten, Endingen, Jechtingen, Ihringen, Oberrotweil and Wasenweiler.

Two further portions of Baden are of something more than passing interest to the wine-drinker, although neither is likely to prove an important factor in the international wine trade for some years to come. Both are in what is called the Ortenau, between Offenburg and Baden-Baden.

The first, directly opposite Strasbourg, and so near that workers in the vineyards can easily see the lone tower of Strasbourg's cathedral in clear weather, consists of a little amphitheater of hills round the village of Durbach, where three enlightened and titled growers produce infinitesimal quantities of a few quite remarkable wines, which generally find so easy and ready a sale among their friends and in the better hotels of Freiburg and Baden-Baden that there is none left for export. The three names, well known to all connoisseurs of *Badische* wine, are Freiherr von Neveu, Graf Wolff-Metternich (this is not the same family as at Schloss Johannisberg) and Schloss Staufenberg, which belongs to the Margrave of Baden. The best wines here come from the Riesling (known sometimes by its local name of Klingelberger), the Traminer and the Ruländer, and a small amount of *Weissherbst* is produced, as on Lake Constance, from the Pinot Noir.

On the north, and just around the corner from Baden-Baden, is what is known as the *Mauerwein* country, where the wines, almost 100% Rieslings, are traditionally shipped in the same sort of Bocksbeutel as the wines of Franconia. Neuweier is the center of this little zone; Varnhalt, Eisental and Steinbach are the other names that one occasionally sees. While hardly distinguished, these have delighted many a traveler in the Black Forest country, and the miniature flagons of Neuweierer, familiar to all visitors to Baden-Baden, are certainly the most engaging and attractive "splits" of still wine that I have ever seen.

3. *Württemberg*

To a person who has never taken the wines of Württemberg very seriously, who remembers vaguely that a good many hillsides along the upper Neckar Valley are covered with vines, and recalls a pleasant glass or two drunk before the War in Stuttgart and Heidelberg, it comes as something of a shock to learn that a single cooperative cellar in Stuttgart now handles the output of over 15,000 acres of vineyard (three times the acreage of the entire Rheingau) and has cellar storage space for over two million bottles. It is a surprise, too, to taste some of the better Württemberger wines that are being produced today, notably by the *Hofkammerkellerei* of the Grand Dukes of Württemberg, by *Graf Adelmann* at Kleinbottwar, by *Graf Neipperg* at Heilbronn and at Schwaigern (where his restaurant, *"Zum Alten Rentamt,"* has acquired a reputation for good food unequaled in Germany) and by the provincial *Lehr- und Versuchsanstalt,* the wine school, at Weinsberg, near Heilbronn.

I should strongly advise the *Landeszentralgenossenschaft Württembergischer Weingartnergenossenschaften e.G.m. b.H.* (for such is the name of the co-op cellar) to come up with a simpler brand name if it ever decides to invade the export market. But the truth is, of course, that most of this is quite ordinary wine, properly destined for local consumption.

Much has been said in the preceding pages of the unfavorable and difficult climate with which German vintners have to contend. The climate of Württemberg is by far the worst of all, so severe that in winter many growers have to take their vines off the wires on which they are strung, bend them over, and cover them with straw or earth to protect them against the cold. Their percentage of good vintages is hardly higher than that of the Saar, but they persist, and endure, and a little of what they make is extraordinarily good.

As might be expected, the best are those made from the classic varieties—Riesling, Traminer, Sylvaner and Ruländer (Pinot Gris), and the notes in my tasting-book read, for a Brussele Traminer 1953, produced at Schloss Schaubeck by Graf Adelmann, "as good a Traminer as I have ever drunk." Of the reds (and I suspect, without having any statistics before me, that there is as much red wine made in Württemberg as white) I can say nothing quite so favorable, but those made from the Trollinger and the Spätburgunder are rather like the reds made round Bolzano, in the Italian Tyrol, fresh, a bit light, somewhat tart and very pleasant.

I am glad to report that *Schillerwein,* that old Württemberger favorite, is on the decline. This is what might be called the step-father of *vin rosé,* a pink or light red wine made from a hodge-podge planting of red grapes and white; its name does not derive, as some have imagined, from the poet Schiller; it comes instead from *schillern,* which is a verb in German and means "shimmer"—however much it shimmered the wine was never much good at its best.

4.   *Mittel-Rhein*

This is a viticultural district of which, despite its spectacular beauty, I can say very little and would as soon leave unsaid what I have to say. In the days when there were no railroads and few roads, when the whole wine trade of Germany depended on the river traffic for its existence, the vineyards, or at least the river towns, of the Mittel-Rhein achieved a quite extraordinary fame. Bacharach and Caub were as celebrated as Johannisberg and Nierstein; both are well north of the fast and dangerous waters of the Binger Loch, which even modern Diesel barges find hard to navigate, and it is safe to assume that both became more famous as centers of the wine trade than distinguished for the wines which their own vineyards produced. For these, today, are decidedly second rate.

Once past Rüdesheim and Bingen, the Rhine heads for the sea. Along its banks, in its deep, almost straight gorge, there is hardly room for the roads and railways along its banks, and for a few, strung-out villages, let alone for vineyards. What vineyards there are seem there by courtesy, terraced up on the slope of a small side valley, half-exposed to the sun on a rocky hill. To one accustomed to see vineyards, it is almost surprising that they produce wine at all.

But they do. And in extremely favorable years, some of the wines are far from bad. It would be unjust not to list them—here are the important wine-producing towns and the better-known *Lagen:*

Oberdiebacher Fürstenberg	Bacharacher Posten
Cauber Blucherthal	Bacharacher Wolfshöhle
Cauber Pfalzgrafenstein	Steeger St. Jost
Cauber Backofen	Steeger Flur
Oberweseler Oelsberg	Steeger Mühlberg
Oberweseler Rheinhell	Bopparder Hamm

5.   *Ahr*

The Ahr is a little river that tumbles down out of the Eifel hills to join the Rhine some fifteen miles south of Bonn. Remagen, near its mouth, had its brief day in the headlines during the War, when its bridge over the Rhine was captured by the American First Army, but it is safe to say that few people outside Germany have ever heard of Walporzheim and Ahrweiler and Neuenahr, or of their wines, or, for that matter, of the Ahr itself. German red wines are not especially preeminent, and the Ahr produces nothing else.

Admittedly, these red wines are as good as any that could be produced at this far northern latitude, nearly three hundred miles farther north than the northernmost corner of Maine; they are made entirely from the Spätburgunder, or Pinot Noir, on tiny terraced hillside plots, and the average holding of some two thousand wine-producing families is under an acre and a half. A large proportion of what they make is drunk up by visitors and tourists, who are as charmed by the valley's intimate and quiet beauty as by its sixteen villages (in the space of sixteen miles), and who would doubtless be glad to buy and drink something much less good than what they get— the completely genuine, fresh, simple "little Burgundies" of the Ahr.

X

RED WINES AND SPARKLING WINES

I DO not know how often, but certainly on many, many
occasions, after a week or a fortnight in Germany, and a succession
of tastings of remarkable and even incomparable white wines, I have
finally ordered and drunk, with what I can only describe as delight
and almost as relief, one of those modest, friendly, small red wines
which German vintners sometimes make in their spare time. Even
the best of these hardly deserves a place on the wine list of a great
restaurant, and there is not one of them that can stand comparison
with the better, let alone the best, red wines of France—in Germany
they are delicious and very welcome.

It is not, I hope, an abuse of hospitality, to suggest that they
should stay at home. There is nothing pleasanter than a Trollinger on
a cool evening in Heilbronn or Stuttgart, and I have drunk Ingelheimer from Rheinhessen and red Dürkheimer from the Pfalz and
Assmannshäuser from the Rheingau and Walporzheimer from the
Ahr Valley, near Bonn, not once but many times and almost always
with real pleasure. But these, to tell the truth, are "country wines"
and they do not "travel."

This is perhaps a ridiculous statement, for of course any properly made wine will "travel," including Vouvray from France, the
wines of Ravello from Italy, those of the Tyrol, and almost all of the
other "doubtful" ones, such as these German reds. It is simply that
away from what the French call their *locale,* their *ambiance,* they
lose their charm, like a nice young cowhand from Wyoming suddenly

127

brought to the city, or wholesome farm cooking served in a New York penthouse. They belong to their own land, and they are never as good as within a mile or two of where they were made.

The most highly regarded German red wines are made from the Pinot Noir grape, which is the great variety of Burgundy, and known in Germany as the *Spätburgunder*. This was brought to the Rhineland, according to tradition, by St. Bernard de Clairvaux, of the Cistercian Order, which has been associated almost since its foundation with vine-growing and with wine. But there are a good many other varieties, of less distinguished origin and less consequence.

Probably the most important of these is called the Portugieser, and seems never to have been properly identified by any other name: its wine is rarely better than fair, but it has the not inconsiderable virtue of being able to survive and prosper and give ripe grapes in the unfavorable climate of the Rhineland. Other varieties include the following: Affenthaler, Limberger, Hängling, Frühburgunder, Urban, most of them completely unknown in other countries.

By all odds the most famous red wine areas of Germany are the Ahr Valley, a tributary of the Rhine between Coblenz and Bonn, and the celebrated State Domain of Assmannshausen, just north of Rüdesheim. Both make their wines from the Pinot Noir, or Spätburgunder, and both wines, at their very summit of excellence, are like rather light and common wines from one of the less famous *communes* of the Burgundian Côte d'Or, or like a good Burgundy of an off year. The best of them is less good than the Pinot Noir from any one of the better producers in California, and there is no possible reason, except sentiment, for shipping them across the Atlantic.

The same thing is certainly true of all the lesser members of the clan—of Ingelheimer and Dürkheimer, of those pleasant, light wines of Württemberg, made from the Trollinger grape, and certainly of those of Baden, although a restaurant owner in Freiburg assured me last summer, that the local red wine was "regarded by all French experts as better than Chambertin."

German sparkling wines suffer inevitably from the same handicaps, and from an even graver one. In all Germany there is not one fine vineyard devoted to the growing of grapes for sparkling wine, and not one fine vineyard where the grapes are used for sparkling wine in any except off years. The best of anything is never a by-product and if Cognac is universally recognized as the best of brandies, and Champagne, from the Champagne district of France, as the greatest of sparkling wines, this is due above all to the fact that in both districts nothing else of the slightest interest or commercial value is made. The grapes from around Rheims and Epernay are grown to make Champagne. German sparkling wines are almost all made from the wines of secondary vineyards, or from the wines of great vineyards in poor years.

Just for example, the whole production of Schloss Johannisberg and Schloss Vollrads, in 1954, was sold to sparkling wine manufacturers, and practically the entire output of the Saar Valley shared the same fate. Disposed of in this way, such wines of great vineyards and off years bring less than half as much, per liter or per barrel, as the wines of good years destined for estate-bottling. This figure is also well below the cost of the raw material of French Champagne.

In good years the producers of *Sekt* or *Schaumwein* (these are the terms most often used—the word "Champagne" being barred by international agreement) go most frequently to the lower Moselle, between Enkirch and Coblenz, and to the extreme upper reaches of the Saar in order to get the less expensive, very light and very tart wines which they require.

Considering these handicaps, and the relatively low price at which it is sold in Germany, the *Sekt* put out by the better houses is quite remarkably good, and its popularity, not only among Germans, but among American officers and tourists, is not surprising. Fortunately the German sparkling wine tax is very low—unlike that in the United States, which is wholly exorbitant—and as a result the vineyard owners have a ready and dependable market for wines that they would otherwise find it difficult to dispose of. Most German sparkling wines, for obvious reasons, do not carry a vintage; some, however, do carry a vineyard name (as Steinberger or Schloss Johannisberger or Scharzberger) and others at least an indication of regional origin and grape variety, as "Saarriesling," a Riesling from the Saar.

The leading producers include the following: Henkell & Co. (Henkell Trocken), Matheus Müller, Sohnlein Rheingold, Deinhard, Kupferberg, Mumm & Co., Schloss Wachenheim, Wilhelm Wasum (Schloss Fürstenburg), etc., etc.

XI

HOW TO BUY AND
STORE GERMAN WINES

Vintage Years Since 1937

SINCE virtually the entire purpose of this little book is to
guide the consumer through the complexities of German wines and
their labels, it seems almost pointless to append a chapter such as this,
and attempt to accomplish, in two or three pages, what I have possibly
failed to achieve in well over a hundred. On the other hand, a brief
summary or round-up can do no harm and may even prove useful, and
a word or two of counsel about buying German wines in the United
States may help to keep the occasional and inevitable disappointments
to a minimum.

It is an unfortunate fact that only a small minority of the owners
of what we call "package stores"—retail dealers in wines and spirits—
in this country, know anything about wine, or have any interest in
learning about it, or have any proper storage facilities for wine, or
care. Those that do—the few—deserve both our patronage and our
gratitude. In their stores, however modest or however large, wines
are displayed and stored with the bottles in their normal, horizontal
position, not set upright, like so many bottles of vinegar, on a shelf,
where the corks will certainly dry out within ninety days, allowing air
to get to the wine and the wine to spoil; at least some effort is made
to keep the space where reserve stocks of wine are stored, reasonably

cool; the proprietor has at least learned to pronounce the names of the wines he offers for sale, and has possibly even tasted some of them, will not offer a Liebfraumilch when asked for a Moselle, and will carry at least a few estate-bottlings of great years. In such stores, and only in such stores, can one buy German wines with a reasonable expectation of getting proper value for what one spends.

German wines, good German wines, are never very cheap even in Germany, and it is folly to imagine that one worth drinking can be had, in America, for much under $2.00, and even this is a very low figure indeed. Below this level, California can provide something a great deal more satisfactory and a great deal more dependable, and California Rieslings are certainly greatly to be preferred to the nondescript Liebfraumilchs on bargain counters. Fine German wines are another matter; they are perhaps not for everyday consumption, but they are capable of providing a pleasure more than commensurate with their cost, always providing they are carefully chosen, genuine beyond question, and have been properly stored.

Few American homes have wine-cellars, and most apartment dwellers can devote at best a closet to the bottles they wish to keep for special occasions and for their discriminating friends. Such a closet is as good as a cellar for all practical purposes, especially for German wines (which do not require long aging), providing the temperature is not over 70° as an average and never, except for very brief periods, over 75°. The wines will mature a little more rapidly than they would, under ideal conditions, underground, but they will not spoil within their normal span of life if stored so that the wine is in contact with the cork. All sorts of convenient and eminently satisfactory wine racks have been designed for such limited storage space, and providing the wines are kept horizontal and reasonably cool, only the purist or the perfectionist will take exception to them. German wines are almost all better when they are relatively young, and most of the talk of cobwebbed bottles and the like is sheer nonsense.

With this disposed of (although I am sure there are still a few old-fashioned gentlemen who will regard such opinions as those of a philistine and an iconoclast, and to them, *Pax*) we may return to the question of buying German wines in the United States.

Perhaps the first point to keep well in mind is that ALL European wines in America seem older than their brother-bottles in Europe, even if originally drawn from the same cask. Everything, except silence and peace and darkness, speeds up the normal aging of a wine—all movement, all handling, all changes in temperature. The famous East India Sherries and the Madeiras which "had twice crossed the line in barrel" were heavily fortified wines which could stand such a voyage, but even these would certainly have been better had they been allowed to grow old more slowly and more gracefully at home. The finer and more delicate wines, such as the Rhines and Moselles, simply cannot stand such treatment. Most European vintage charts of course do not take these factors into account, and it is safe to assume that many wines which they call "not yet ready," are quite ready here. This is particularly the case with regard to German wines, whose freshness and fruit make up so large a part of their charm. Almost all of them are better here when they are five years old or less, and they rarely improve very much, once they are imported, even when properly kept. No German wine, except a rare and extraordinary estate-bottling, should be bought if it is, or if it claims to be, over seven or eight years old, and five years, on the whole, is a sounder deadline.

Next come a whole series of points which have been made sufficiently clear in the preceding chapters. At the risk of seeming to insist on the obvious, let me say (or repeat):

1.   The better German wines carry the name of a specific town (with a few rare exceptions) plus that of a vineyard.

2.   The better German wines are natural wines, made without the addition of sugar, and can be recognized as such if one cares to take the trouble.

3.   The better German wines are estate-bottled and are clearly so marked—clearly, that is, to anyone who knows the specific terms used to indicate estate-bottling.

4.   The higher grades of German wines all carry special and legally-defined indications which are accurate as to their character and class.

A cursory second glance at Chapter II, including the Glossary at its end and what comes in the following pages, should be sufficient in the way of signposts for any real wine-lover and wine-enthusiast to find his way.

Here is a brief commentary on recent vintage years in German wines. The numerical ratings are based on the principle that 20/20 is perfection, 12/20 hardly passing, and 10/20 and below, something that most of us would just as soon forget. The ratings are based on the present quality of the wines in question, not on their original worth during, what was for many of them, their brief days of glory:

VINTAGE CHART

1965. *Evaluation as of September, 1965*: Almost certainly poor.

1964. Great, but with a considerable number of exceptions and reservations. The crop was extremely large, and, as is often the case in overly copious years, the cheaper wines (especially those that have been *verbesserte,* or sugared) are flat and dull, lack sprightliness and freshness and charm; they will be short lived, rate perhaps 12/20. On the other hand, the best wines of the Saar and Ruwer and some from the Moselle are quite extraordinary—fragrant and fruity and ripe like the 1953s, and deserve 17/20 at least. The Rheingaus are perhaps a shade less fine, though the best since 1959. 16/20. Other German wines somewhat low in acid, not too attractive. 14/20.

1963. Good but uneven. Quite remarkable sugared wines were made, particularly in the Ruwer, Saar and Rheingau, and some surprisingly fine *Naturweine* by almost all the top producers, everywhere. The best rate 15/20 but there are many thin and poor ones as well.

1962. Good, quite comparable to '63 and '61, best in the Rheingau. Fresh, charming, will not last. 14/20.

1961. Good, although far from the magnificent vintage that this year proved in France. More and better *natur* wines were produced than in 1963 and 1962; light, agreeable, on the dry side, these matured quickly. 15/20.

1960. Poor. Now generally off the market. 10/20.

1959. An exceedingly great year, unsurpassed since the last war, comparable to 1921 in quality. The lesser wines are of course past their prime and off the market; the best are just now reaching their peak and will hold for at least a decade. This is particularly true of the Saar, the Ruwer, of selected Moselles like those of Wehlen and of a few Rheingaus, all of which deserve 19/20.

1958. A sound secondary vintage no longer available. 13/20.

1957. A few *Spitzenweine* have survived; the others, no.

1956. Very poor. Gone.

1955. Once good. A few Moselles have survived, rate 13/20.

1954.   One of the worst.

1953.   A great year: wines of immense finesse and charm in their
youth, now too old. 12/20 to 14/20.

Wines older than the 1953s are in general unprocurable. One is occasionally privileged to taste, from producers' and collectors' cellars,
rare and precious wines of 1949, 1945, 1937 and even 1921. Stored
under ideal conditions, many of them are remarkable even now, but
they are a small and vanishing band of survivors, all their contemporaries gone with the snows of yesteryear.

XII

SERVING AND TASTING
GERMAN WINES

I T IS an odd fact, although not a very surprising one, that the
wine countries of the world tend to produce wines that go well with
the better dishes of their national cuisine. At first glance there appear
to be a few important and obvious exceptions to this rule: nothing
could be worse with Portuguese food than Port—but of course Port
is hardly ever drunk in Portugal, and amounts to less than 3% of the
annual wine production of that happy and thirsty little country. Similarly Sherry, which no one would think of ordering with a *paella* or a
cocido, is anything but the national wine of Spain—the Spaniards
produce 45 gallons of table wine for every gallon of Sherry, they drink
practically all of the former, and export most of the latter.

But it would be hard to conceive of French cooking without
French wine, and Italian wine is a fitter companion to Italian food
than any French wine would be. What the Spaniards and Portuguese
drink (unlike what they sell) is agreeable with what they eat, and
California is tending, more and more, to produce the kind of light,
dry, pleasant, simple wines which go hand in hand with our traditional roast turkey and fried chicken and steak.

The one really bona fide exception is Germany. It is possible to
eat very well in Germany, but few if any of the typical and characteristic German dishes really call for wine—particularly the sort of
fragrant, delicate, flowery wine which the better Moselle and Rhine
vineyards produce. Whatever the *Feinschmecker* may tell us, there

135

are certainly better things to eat with Marcobrunner or with Wehlener Sonnenuhr than sausage with sauerkraut or paprika Schnitzel or liver dumplings or pork chops or Sauerbraten or Hasenpfeffer. These, if anything, go with the more common wines of Württemberg and Baden, or with beer. The Germans, as a matter of fact, drink many of their best wines between meals, on a terrace, on a sunny summer afternoon, or in the evening after dinner, and of all the light wines of the world the Moselles and Rhines are certainly the most agreeable so served. There do exist, furthermore, a few German dishes (though not exclusively or typically German) which go magnificently with wine—trout from the Black Forest or the Eifel, cooked *au bleu* (*Blauforellen*), crayfish (*Krebs*), salmon from the Rhine (*Rheinsalm*) or tench (*Schleie*), chicken, if cooked simply, or cold cuts, which are generally excellent. But perhaps the truth of the matter is that German wines, like German music, do not really belong to Germany but to the world.

In considering the service of German wines, it is essential to remember that some German wines, including all of the rarest and most expensive, are somewhat sweet. These should no more be served before a red wine, a Burgundy, for example, than Château d'Yquem should be served before Château Latour, or than chocolate pudding should precede roast beef. This category includes all *Beerenauslesen* and *Trockenbeerenauslesen,* and even a few *Auslesen* of exceedingly great years; these are dessert wines, and their place is with dessert, or with a snack, or no food at all, in the late evening.

There is a middle category—wines that have a trace of sweetness but are not truly sweet. Such are most of the *Auslesen,* especially those of the Moselle and many of the Rheingau; they are not very flattering to a red wine that follows them, but are admirable if served as the single wine with a meal when the principal *plat* is veal, or fowl, or fish, or almost anything with a cream sauce, or cold meat or cold lobster.

Lastly there are the wines of up to and including *Spätlese* rank, and many *Auslesen* from the Moselle. The Germans serve wines of this sort with everything, including red meat and game, but to do so is generally to do an injustice to a good dish and a good bottle, for the two simply do not go together. Naturally, however, one's own taste must be the final arbiter, and all that it is possible to do here is to hint at the accumulated experience of a great many people who have liked both fine food and fine wine. German wines of this class (and this is the class that most experts, and most people, prefer, even if they gladly recognize the superiority of the sweeter and the rarer) can be served before a red wine, or before a greater and sweeter white wine, or straight through a meal where white wine is called for. Obviously, if more than one German wine is served, the lighter (Moselle) should precede the heavier (Rhine), and the dryer precede the sweeter.

As far as temperature is concerned, Germans generally serve their wines less cold than what is considered standard practice in France or England or the United States. If the wine comes from a cool cellar, they often do not use an ice-bucket at all, and drink it cheerfully and appreciatively at about 60° Fahrenheit. This is anything but damaging, possibly even helpful, to a great wine, less so to a good or fair one; but American dining rooms, in winter as in summer, are considerably warmer than German ones by and large, and most of us will prefer German wines chilled to about 52° to 55°. Unfortunately, most of our manufacturers of wine-buckets follow the French tradition, and as a result the wine in the neck of a German bottle is above the ice and is not chilled in a bucket at all. In such cases, it is perfectly good practice to put the bottle neck-down in the bucket for ten minutes or so before it is brought to the table; there being no sediment, the wine is not injured in the least. Of course it is even better and much simpler to put the bottle in an electric refrigerator for approximately an hour before serving. It goes without saying that the top of the lead capsule should be cut off, and the rim of the bottle wiped clean before the cork is drawn.

Like all other good wines, Moselles and Rhines should be served preferably in clear, thin, stemmed glasses. They are prettier so, and they taste better. The traditional form is a sort of flat cup, with straight or in-curving sides, mounted on a tall stem, but a tulip shape is certainly as good, and in any case the glasses should not be filled much over half full. The so-called *Pokal* or *Römer* (a goblet mounted on a cone-shaped stem) is only used in Germany for the most ordinary wine; it generally holds either ¼ or ½ liter, and is filled to the brim. Fine wines are never so served.

Since there is no real reason for buying or serving or drinking a fine wine, whether German or French or American, except the pleasure that it gives, it seems wholly nonsensical not to take the small additional trouble to taste it carefully and get a maximum of enjoyment out of something so carefully made to provide precisely that.

Far too much has been said and written about "tasting" wine, as if the matter involved some exceedingly complex procedure or technique. This is all very well for professionals, who are often asked to grade and price a hundred or more wines in a morning, who perforce must spit out what they taste, at the risk of misgrading half of the samples, who are highly paid for the job and regard it as very hard work indeed. This is not the way to enjoy wine, nor to taste it when one is drinking it. Basically, the one real essential, whether one has had a cocktail before, or two, or none, whether one smokes or not, whether the menu has been planned to "bring out" the wine, or not—the one real essential is to devote at least a moment or two of undivided attention to the wine one drinks. It is no more possible to judge and appreciate and fully enjoy a wine while carrying on a lively conversation on some other subject than to judge a pianist's performance, or appreciate a good play, or even watch and enjoy a football game under similar conditions. The concentration required to judge and enjoy a wine involves perhaps a minute, certainly less than three—a brief space to inhale and weigh the bouquet or aroma, a few seconds to take a sip or two and hold the wine in one's mouth while inhaling and then exhaling, then just the time to judge and enjoy the aftertaste.

An expert can tell a great deal about a wine by its color, but this is not easy for the amateur since such judgments have to be based on a great deal of experience and a very accurate memory for fine shades. It is possible to say that all German wines, except the very great and sweet ones, should be pale gold, with a certain amount of green in their make-up, as transparent as water, and so brilliant that they shine in their glass either in lamplight or in sunlight. The greater and sweeter wines are gold, not green, and when they begin to show a coppery tinge, they are reaching the end of their career. The Moselles, of course, are the palest of all.

In German wines the question of bouquet is primary and all-important. But the special, recognizable and characteristic bouquet which certain wines possess, cannot be described; it is as subtle and evanescent as the scent of a flower. Nevertheless, it is not difficult to distinguish, on the basis of bouquet alone, between a great and a fairly good and a poor German wine, nor does one have to be any sort of expert to tell a Moselle from a Rhine wine, *providing* one can sniff them comparatively at a single tasting. The faculty which permits a professional taster to give a wine's class, and often name the township and precise vineyard which produced it, is much less a

matter of talent and aptitude than of long practice and taste memory.
It requires, of course, a high degree of concentration.

A wine's bouquet is most apparent and can be best appreciated
when it is not too cold, when it is served in large glasses filled to no
more than a third of their capacity, and when the wine has been
swirled or shaken in the glass before it is brought to the nose. This
swirling and shaking, which looks rather ridiculous to the uninitiated,
is anything but silly—the entire inner surface of the tulip-shaped
glass becomes thus coated with wine and serves as a sort of chimney,
concentrating the wine's aroma and channeling it upwards, and just
as any carbonated liquid tends to give off its bubbles when it is
shaken, so a wine gives off its bouquet when it is moved.

Even to a complete beginner, the bouquet of a fine wine is immediately more agreeable than that of a small, common, or poor one.
Of course there are pitfalls and one can make mistakes. The odor and
taste of sulphur (which generally makes itself known by a slight
prickling in the nose, and an odd, almost indescribable, faintly "pasty"
impression on the tip of the tongue) is so common in cheap German
wines that I have actually seen fine German wines criticized, by
Germans, because they had none of it. It is also possible to mistake
the first, early traces of maderization, or oxidation, or old age, for
something much better—the bouquet of a great wine, still sound; all
wines, especially white wines, tend to develop a special bloom before
they die, and acquire a sort of false funereal beauty which is immensely attractive on first acquaintance; let them stand half an hour
in their glass, and you will readily recognize them for what they are.
The elements to look for in the bouquet of a fine German wine are,
principally, fruit and breed. Neither is easy to describe. The wine
should have a scent as definite as that of a very ripe peach or plum
or quince or strawberry, though very different from these, and a good
deal more complex, so that you find yourself baffled when you try to
define it in terms of anything else. It should be even more interesting
and even more baffling when you sniff it for the tenth time, with
nothing in its make-up which you could describe as heavy or fatiguing
or flat. But these are only words.

Taste and aftertaste can only be judged and appreciated in the
same way, and only described in equally vague terms. Both should be
wholly agreeable if the wine is good, and any trace of anything else
should render a wine immediately suspect. Both should be in keeping
with the wine's bouquet (the aftertaste of a too old wine is generally

not) and both, basically, should be appetizing, so that you are left sorry that there is not more in the bottle, and reluctant to drink the last drops in your glass. This, essentially, is the proof of a fine wine.

German wine tasters, like technicians in special fields the world over, have a special jargon of their own. Here, in brief and necessarily inadequate translation, are most of the terms they use.

A BRIEF LIST OF GERMAN WINE-TASTING TERMS

ansprechend	Prepossessing and attractive.
Art	Character. A noun, almost always used with a modifying adjective, generally a favorable one.
blumig	With bouquet.
bitter	As in English.
Bodengeschmack, Bodenton	An earthy taste, easy to recognize but hard to describe, often found in common wines grown on heavy soil.
breit	Uninteresting. Neutral and dull.
bukettreich	Having a pronounced and agreeable bouquet.
dick	Coarse and common.
duftig	Fragrant. Delicate, with fine bouquet.
dünn	Thin and watery.
edel	Noble. Distinguished and out of the ordinary.
elegant	Having unusual finesse and class.
faul	Moldy.
fein	Fine, as in English.
firn	Old, in the sense of maderized or oxidized, past its prime.
fluchtig	Light and inconsequential. Not much to it.
frisch	Fresh, in the sense of refreshing and agreeable.
fruchtig	Fruity. With fresh, definitely agreeable bouquet and flavor.

Fülle	Richness. Applied only to great wines.
gefullt	Rich and full.
gering	Poor. A strong term.
gezuckert	A wine made with the addition of sugar, not necessarily sweet.
glatt	Smooth and pleasing.
gross	Big and good. Can also mean great.
grün	Green, in the sense of unmature, unready.
gut	Good, as in English.
harmonisch	Well rounded and balanced. Not necessarily great. A favorable term.
Hefegeschmack	A yeasty wine, or one that has the taste of lees. In almost all cases, the result of careless cellar work.
herb	Bitter or astringent.
hochedel	Superb and noble. Applicable only to the best.
Holzgeschmack	A woody flavor, due to a bad barrel or careless cellar work.
hübsch	Pretty or nice. Can be said of a pleasant lesser wine, not of a great one.
jung	Young. Just that.
kernig	Sturdy, possibly without finesse or fruit.
klein	Small, without much body or flavor.
Körper	Body. Means just that.
kräftig	Big, robust, high in alcohol.
kurz	Short. Not much flavor and no aftertaste.
mager	Poor, thin. A common wine with nothing to recommend it.
milde	Pleasantly soft, possibly a little sweet, sometimes lacking in character and distinction.

natur	A natural and authentic wine made without the addition of sugar.
pikant	Intriguing and appetizing—the opposite of dull. High praise.
rassig	Having distinction and breed.
rauh	Raw or harsh.
reif	Ripe and fine, possibly somewhat sweet. High praise.
rein	Clean. Also means unsugared, a natural wine.
reintönig	Sound and well-balanced.
rund	Round, well-balanced, complete.
saftig	Succulent, agreeable, often a wine with low acid.
sauber	Clean and sound, with no "off" taste.
scharf	Undergoing secondary fermentation, not in good condition, "off"—an unfavorable term.
schimmelig	Moldy or musty.
schön	Lovely, charming, attractive, not necessarily great.
Schwefel	Sulphur. All too often present in lesser German wines. See page 139.
schwer	Heavy, full-bodied, without finesse.
Spiel	Unusual character. A noun.
spritzig	Very faintly, sometimes almost imperceptibly, sparkling.
stahlig	Steely—means hard, somewhat austere.
stoffig	Substantial, with good body, full.
süffig	Palatable, easy to drink.
süss	Sweet. Means just that.
trocken	Dry, withered, lacking in freshness and fruit. A generally unfavorable term when applied to still wines.

voll	Full. With plenty of body, but not too much. A favorable term.
vornehm	Well rounded and balanced. Not necessarily great. A favorable term.
weich	Weak, soft and flat.
weinig	Definite character, good balance. Nevertheless, not too flattering a term.
würzig	Spicy. Attractive in bouquet and flavor. High praise.
zart	Tender, light and delicate.
Zukunft	Future. A wine that has Zukunft is one that will improve.

NOTES

NOTE 1-1　PAGE 11

Over the past decade, especially since the uneven and rather difficult 1957 vintage, there has been a steady trend in Germany in favor of a less rigid and more practical attitude toward the sugaring or *chaptalization* of lesser wines. This has partly been due to an effort to bring the German and French wine laws into closer accord—in the interest, hopefully, of a future Common Market. Since almost all Burgundies are chaptalized, even in great years, and most Bordeaux in secondary vintages like 1956, 1960, 1963 and 1965 (without bearing any indication of this fact on the label), many of the best German producers have come to feel that they, too, might legitimately follow a somewhat similar procedure—sugar and ferment and age and bottle their own lesser wines, especially in poorer years. In the past, instead, they had sold either the grapes or the new-made wine to shippers, for handling and blending.

This decision taken, a number of the largest and best vineyard owners have ceased to be members of the prestigious *Verband Deutscher Naturwein-Versteigerer* (*see* Page 27). They have devised special labels for these sugared wines, differing in some degree from the labels used on their *Naturweine,* and have put them on the market at very reasonable prices. So far, the experiment seems to have been a resounding success, with everyone, except possibly the commercial shippers, gaining greatly thereby. The wines are almost invariably far superior to the commercial blends in which they were formerly drowned, and if they are a little more expensive than these, they are well worth what they cost. They never, of course, carry such designations as *Wachstum, Original-Abfüllung,* or *Natur* (let alone *Kabinett* or *Spätlese*) but they have their full share of bouquet and breed, and are hardly distinguishable from *Naturweine,* even by an expert taster. Major wine-growers who now produce and sell such wines, most of which can be unhesitatingly recommended, include, in the Mosel-Saar-Ruwer: Von Schubert, of Maximin-Grünhaus, and the Friedrich-Wilhelm Gymnasium; in the Rheingau, Schloss Eltz, Schloss Reinhartshausen, Schloss Groensteyn, Freiherr Langwerth von Simmern; in Rheinhessen, Franz-Karl Schmitt.

There is one odd characteristic of these wines—so odd that it is almost incredible—which should nevertheless be kept firmly in mind: *they are immeasurably better in bad vintages than in good*; in very great years, such as 1959, they are either nearly worthless, or do not exist at all. The reasons are neither mysterious nor absurd.

1. Being producer-bottled, the vintages they carry are completely authentic, something which is a long way from being true of all, or even most, commercial wines.

2. In great years, these best vineyards produce *no* wine that has to be *verbesserte,* or sugared, and in good years very little. At Maximin-Grünhaus, for example, the von Schuberts produced in 1964 *no* sugared wine considered worthy of their name and label, while in 1963 a large proportion of the crop was sugared, and was of admirable quality in its class. All of the good 1964 was *Naturwein.*

3. Outstanding vineyards, even in poor years, show their basic superiority, and even if their grapes are deficient in sugar and their wines chaptalized, maintain to a surprisingly large degree their breed and class and general excellence. If bottled by the grower, such wines are almost always better values than commercial bottlings, whatever vintage the latter may flaunt.

There are perhaps a few additional points which should be made here, insufficiently covered in the first edition, which have become increasingly important over the years. It had been hoped that the Common Market discussions would resolve these, but no such solution now seems likely in the immediate future. Briefly, under certain specified conditions and within certain legal limits, one may add water as well as sugar, in Germany, to what is to be sold as wine. This is a practice as old as wine making, authorized and necessary in some colder countries (including New York State as well as Germany), forbidden in others where it is unnecessary (including California, Spain, Italy, and most of France). Vintners in these northern districts must in many autumns deal with grapes which are not only too low in sugar but too high in acid to yield a generally salable natural wine, as almost all Concord grapes, for example. The sugar deficiency can be dealt with by adding sugar, as discussed above, but a reduction of excess acidity is best and most naturally achieved by what is known as gallisation, or adding water, which of course gives more "wine" per ton of grapes, and leads to abuses unless rigidly controlled.

The laws are not by any means as strict as they should be and their enforcement even less so in this particular respect. Many producers of German *Sekt,* or sparkling wine, and most shippers of very cheap German table wine— the Liebfraumilch and Zeller Schwarze Katz (alas! quite often some more honorable names as well) — that one finds on bargain counters, buy, to produce what they sell, the most acid grapes or young wines they can find, and for all too obvious reasons.

While it may be said that the end result of all this is to give the eventual consumer something quite healthful, which he likes and is willing to pay for, it is certainly true that he should be told what he is getting.

NOTE 1-2   PAGE 14

An additional category, once regarded as hardly more than a curiosity, has begun to attract some public interest and has acquired some commercial importance of late. Called *Eiswein,* this is a rare oddity which could almost be considered an accidental *Auslese*; it is made from the first pressing of frozen grapes. In certain vintage seasons in Germany severe night frosts are not uncommon and temperatures as low as 20° Fahrenheit are recorded in the vineyards. When pickers arrive at sunrise, the less ripe grapes with lower sugar content are frozen solid, but the overripe grapes with sweeter juice are only partially frozen. If brought to the *Kelterhaus* and pressed, the first run of the juice comes almost entirely from the ripest berries and this, if fermented separately, is *Eiswein.* The result is a rather sweet, interesting wine, usually less well-balanced and considerably less fine than a true *Auslese.*

NOTE 2-1   PAGE 22

Laws and regulations covering the labeling of wine hardly even existed a hundred years ago, and although immense progress has been made, it is not surprising that they still leave a good deal to be desired. From the consumer's point of view (and the protection of the consumer is their only reason for existence) they often seem surprisingly vague and lax, just in those areas where the wine-drinker would wish to see them especially precise and stringent. This is no less (and no more) true in Germany than in France, the United States, and all other wine-producing countries.

Oddly enough, the strong points in the national wine laws of one country are often the grave weaknesses in the regulations of its neighbor, and it is greatly to be hoped that if the Common Market discussions are ever resumed and arrive at an accord, they will produce a uniform set of much stricter rules.   ◦

Thus in France and Germany, with the unique and notable exception of château and estate-bottlings, many, even most "vintage" wines contain a substantial admixture of the wine of some other year. The same thing is true in Italy and Spain, but is rigidly prohibited in the United States.

On the other hand, our legalized malpractices are no less flagrant: an American "Rhine Wine" or "Burgundy" can be made anywhere, out of any kind of grapes; California "Chablis" and "Sauterne" are drawn, as often as not, out of the same tank. And even our best, our *varietal* wines, sold as "Johannisberg Riesling" and "Pinot Noir," need be no more than 51% the product of the noble grape varieties whose names they bear, the other 49% being made quite lawfully from who-knows-what. All of which would be highly illegal and quite inconceivable abroad.

In Germany (again with the unique and notable exception of producer-bottlings, including not only *Original-Abfüllung* wines but the special *verbesserte* wines dealt with in Note 1-1 above) wide abuses are now permitted in the use of what the consumer might reasonably assume to be geographical names. Providing the wine is of "equal quality and value" (the shipper being the sole judge) a wine may be sold under a village name if the grapes were grown within 9 airline miles (15 kilometers) of the village in question. This means that a commercial "Piesporter" need no longer come from Piesport but may have been produced in some obscure nearby township such as Mehring or Thörnisch; that a shipper's "Rüdesheimer" and "Johannisberger" may be identical and both grown on some undistinguished hillside 20 miles away by road. The French system of *"Appellations Contrôlées"* if ever applied in Germany, would eliminate all this, just as the German rules governing the labeling of sugared vs. non-sugared wines would be of great help to the consumer of French wines, if applied in France.

What is even more serious, in Germany, is the official blessing recently given to a system of what are known as *Gattungslagen,* which can be roughly translated as "generic vineyard names." The use of these is governed by a mass of complex rules which no officialdom will be able to enforce and no consumer to understand. Fortunately, they do not affect estate-bottlings, which is one more reason for sticking to these whenever possible. Briefly, the net result is to reclassify, downgrade, and place practically in the public domain, dozens of *Lagenamen* which wine-drinkers have thought applicable only to the wines of a specific given vineyard, so that henceforth they will have hardly any geographical meaning at all.

Certain *Lagen,* or vineyards, will have their names protected as before— those of which the boundaries are set down in the official land register (*Kataster*), and those which have acquired over the years a traditional or historic meaning (*Volkmundslagen*). But no indication of all this need appear on the label: the consumer must be his own policeman and his own guide.

Below is a *partial* list of what are *now Gattungslagen.* Unless estate-bottled, their wines need not come from the vineyard whose name they bear:

Saar
Niedermenniger Euchariusberg
Oberemmeler Scharzberg
Saarburger Schlossberg
Scharzberger
Wiltinger Scharzberg

Mosel
Bernkasteler Braunes
Graacher Braunes
Graacher Münzlay
Niederemmeler Michelsberg
Piesporter Michelsberg
Wehlener Münzlay
Wehlener Bickert
Uerziger Schwarzlay
Zeltinger Schwarzlay

Rheinhessen
Aslheimer Goldberg
Binger Rosengarten
Bodenheimer Hohberg
Dienheimer Goldberg
Nackenheimer Fritzenhölle
Niersteiner Fritzenhölle
Niersteiner Schnappenberg
Oppenheimer Goldberg
Oppenheimer Kröttenbrunnen

Rheingau
Eltviller Sandgrube
Eltviller Pellet
Eltviller Steinmächer
Eltviller Wagenkehr
Erbacher Pellet
Erbacher Kiesling
Geisenheimer Steinacker
Hallgartener Deutelsberg
Hallgartener Mehrhölchen
Hochheimer Daubhaus
Johannisberger Erntebringer
Kiedricher Sandgrube
Oestricher Deez
Rauenthaler Steinmächer
Rüdesheimer Häuserweg
Rüdesheimer Kiesel
Winkeler Erntebringer
Winkeler Oberberg

Rheinpfalz
Deidesheimer Grundpfad
Deidesheimer Neuberg
Deidesheimer Hofstück
Dürkheimer Feuerberg
Dürkheimer Spielberg
Dürkheimer Michelsberg
Forster Altenburg
Forster Hahnenböhl
Forster Langenböhl
Rupperstberger Hofstück
Ruppertsberger Mühlweg
Wachenheimer Altenburg
Wachenheimer Neuberg

NOTE 3-1   PAGE 37

As has been pointed out in the Preface to this Revised Edition, the past ten years have brought profound changes to the Moselle Valley—its landscape and its whole character as well. The silvery, rippling little river, with its reedy banks and its oddly Arcadian charm, is gone, never to return. In its place, the new canal, consisting of a chain of long, narrow, winding lakes, separated by locks, carries the deep-bellied coal barges of the Ruhr up to the foundries of French Lorraine, and the iron ore of Lorraine back, via the Rhine, to Essen. New bridges have replaced most the old, primitive cable ferries. The Moseltalbahn, or "drunkards' railway line," now runs from Trier only as far as Neumagen, and its days are numbered; wide new roads have replaced many of the old, narrow, winding ones, and there are excursion steamers and a good many outboard motorboats on the river.

There are a few changes in the vineyards too. Diagonal roads have been cut, zig-zag fashion, up through the vines, so tractors bring up the loads that the vintners formerly and for nearly twenty centuries, carried on their backs, and similarly bring down the grapes at harvest time.

NOTE 4-1 PAGE 69

I am glad although slightly abashed to report that I at last know the answe to this question of "Marcobrunner" vs. "Erbacher Markobrunn." I should hav guessed it long since. Growers whose vines are mostly in the Erbach half o this incomparable vineyard (which purists seem to regard as the senior line) use "Erbacher Markobrunn;" those in the Hattenheim section (whose wines, over the years, I have found that I prefer) call their wines "Marcobrunner." This difference, let us hope, need not lead to public violence or to family feuds.

NOTE 4-2 PAGE 74

As I have written elsewhere, in my *Encyclopedia of Wine,* the labels and capsules of Schloss Vollrads, "make up what is perhaps the most complicated hierarchy . . . in the whole, often complicated, world of wine." Just to add a few additional hazards to an already difficult course, the various capsule colors sometimes change rank, or are eliminated, and larger buyers are occasionally allowed to overprint, on the Schloss label, some private designation of their own, such as a large yellow chevron, of which only the buyer and Graf Matuschka know the precise meaning. I have even seen the word "Spätlese" overprinted on such, though without authorization.

What follows I believe is accurate for the moment:
1. The least expensive Schloss Vollrads carry the Schloss label, and the words *Original-Abfüllung.* There are, in this category, six grades. The three lowest wear a green capsule . . . the Pfc (for all this is perhaps best explained in military terminology) green alone, the Corporal, green-with-a-silver-stripe, the Sergeant, green-with-a-gold-stripe. We then have, supposedly from a better regiment with red capsules, red alone, red-with-silver, red-with-gold.
2. A bit better still, although the difference is by no means a giant step, are the wines that carry the Schloss Vollrads label plus the word *Schlossabzug.* Here, too, we have green and red capsules, with silver and gold stripes indicating higher rank, and in precisely the same order.
3. To move over into what might be called "officers' country," we have the Vollrads equivalent of Spätlese, which is *Kabinett.* And once more, but with a blue capsule, we get blue, blue-with-silver, blue-with-gold.
4. The details of the Auslesen, etc. are still accurate as given on page 75.

NOTE 4-3 PAGE 76

I have been personally assured by Paul von Metternich that Schloss Johannisberg was *at no time* used as an observation post during World War II, and he, if anyone, should know. This is far from the first time that bombardiers have told tall stories, but, considering the risks and perils of their employment, who can blame them?

INDEX